The Goal of Full Employment

The Goal of Full Employment

ROBERT AARON GORDON

One of a series of books from
The Research Program on Unemployment
Institute of Industrial Relations
University of California, Berkeley

JOHN WILEY & SONS, INC.

NEW YORK   LONDON   SYDNEY

Preface

This monograph is one of a series of volumes resulting from the research program on Unemployment and the American Economy which has been carried on at the University of California. The work was made possible by a generous grant from the Ford Foundation to the Institute of Industrial Relations on the Berkeley campus.[1]

When this program began in 1962, there was widespread and deep concern over the persisting high level of unemployment in the United States. The year 1962 was the fifth consecutive year in which unemployment had remained above 5 per cent. The goal of full employment seemed far away. Not until the year 1966 did the average annual unemployment rate fall below 4 per cent, for the first time since 1953. The rate had been a little above 4 per cent in the prosperous years, 1955 to 1957.

Like all of the other advanced economies of the Western world, the United States has accepted "full employment" as one of the goals of national economic policy. How is this goal to be defined—not only in terms of an overall rate of unemployment but also in terms of an acceptable pattern of unemployment rates when the labor force is classified by age, sex, color, occupation, and other significant characteristics? And how is the goal of

[1] The program was originally under the direction of Arthur M. Ross and myself. Since the fall of 1965, Mr. Ross has been on leave to serve as U.S. Commissioner of Labor Statistics.

full employment to be reconciled with other economic goals with which it may conflict—for example, the goal of price stability? These are the kinds of questions with which the present study is concerned. Or, to state the matter differently, we are concerned in this volume with formulating for the United States the goal of full employment in both *aggregative* and *structural* terms.

We make considerable use (particularly in Chapters 5 and 6) of the official data on unemployment as published by the U. S. Bureau of Labor Statistics. For the most part, these data extend only through 1965, since annual figures for 1966 were not available at the time the study was completed. Beginning in January 1967 the BLS adopted several definitional changes, and some of the unemployment data for preceding years have been revised to reflect at least one of these changes: the elimination of 14- and 15-year-olds from the labor force. It is estimated that the changes affect the unemployment rate by not more than 0.2 per cent in either direction. Therefore the data presented here (in Chapters 1, 5, and 6) based on the old definitions, probably would not be significantly changed if they were revised to conform to the new definitions.[2]

I am happy to acknowledge my indebtedness to several persons. My wife, Margaret S. Gordon, and Stephan F. Kaliski read the manuscript and offered a number of helpful suggestions. I leaned heavily on my research assistants, Ruth Parker, Günter Wittich, and David Kotz. Barbara Palmer typed the manuscript, including the many elaborate tables, and otherwise helped in bringing this project to completion.

R. A. GORDON

June 1967

[2] The effect of the revisions for the year 1966 are explored in some detail in a set of tables in the February 1967 issue of *Employment and Earnings and Monthly Report on the Labor Force,* published by the U.S. Bureau of Labor Statistics.

Contents

The Goal of Full Employment

CHAPTER 1

The Facts and the Issues

There can be little argument with the statement that "The United States has long since decided that high employment is an important national objective and that the government has a responsibility for its achievement."[1] The official commitment to the goal of high employment was made in the Employment Act of 1946, and there has been no visible effort, by either Republicans or Democrats, to withdraw that commitment since then. In February 1964, that commitment was dramatically reaffirmed by the United States Congress when it voted the largest tax reduction in American history.

In passing the Employment Act, Congress was careful to avoid using the then controversial phrase "full employment," although it was not afraid to say that "it is the continuing policy and responsibility of the Federal Government . . . to promote *maximum* employment, production, and purchasing power."[2] A decade and a half later, the Commission on National Goals appointed by President Eisenhower apparently felt no compunction in referring to "our goal of full employment."[3] And even more recently, Arthur F. Burns, the highly respected president of the National Bureau of Economic Research and first Chairman of the Council of Economic Advisers in the Eisenhower Administration, felt moved to say that, "I believe that the American people are more firmly committed to the ideal of full employment than they were a generation ago. If the Employment Act were recast today, it might even be christened 'The Full Employment Act,' as was the original Murray bill."[4]

Whichever adjective—"high," "maximum," "full," or some other—suits our particular taste, it is clear that the United States, like all the other industrially advanced countries of the Western world, has committed itself to some sort of employment policy, to taking steps to insure that "there will be afforded useful employment opportunities, including self-employment, for those able, willing, and seeking to work . . . ."[5]

The obverse of employment is, of course, unemployment. A policy of high, maximum, or full employment implies a policy which keeps unemployment at a satisfactorily low level, although there is always room for disagreement as to what is "satisfactorily low." Indeed, the success of an employment policy is almost always judged by what happens to the level or rate of unemployment.

What level and pattern of unemployment in the United States corresponds to "full" or "maximum" or satisfactorily high employment? This is the question with which this study is primarily concerned. Or, to put the question another way, how should we formulate an employment policy for the United States in terms of both the *level* and the *structure* of unemployment that we would consider to be satisfactory?

The Unemployment Record

Whatever the answers we eventually suggest, it is clear that, by any reasonable criterion, total unemployment in the United States has not been at a satisfactorily low level during most of the period since World War II. Furthermore, there would be general agreement that the burden of unemployment has been very unevenly and inequitably distributed. We have had to worry not only about unemployment in the aggregate but also about the structure of unemployment.

Let us first examine total unemployment. A widely used criterion is a national unemployment rate of 4 per cent. This is the "interim target" set by President Kennedy's Council of Economic Advisers and, in effect, the target accepted by the Council under President Eisenhower. The latter's Commission on National Goals, to cite another example, stated that "we must seek to keep unemployment consistently below 4 per cent of the labor force."[6]

Table 1.1 suggests how seriously we have failed to achieve this goal over the last twenty years. For seven consecutive years, from 1958 through 1964, the unemployment rate on an annual basis remained above 5 per cent.[7] It was at or below 4 per cent only during the boom following World War II and during the forced-draft years of the Korean War, 1951–1953. The prosperity of the mid-fifties yielded annual unemployment rates of 4.2–4.4 per cent. At the time this book was being written, it appeared that, for the first time in a decade, 1966 would yield an annual unemployment rate of just about—or perhaps a bit below—4 per cent.

But are we wise to put this much emphasis on a single unemployment figure for the labor force as a whole—which gives the same weight to teen-agers in school looking for part-time work as it does to married men who must have jobs to support their families? More often than not, the question is framed so as to imply its own answer—that the overall unemployment rate gives an exaggerated impression of the hardship which results from unemployment.

There is no question that too much public attention is focused on the single unemployment figure for the entire labor force. This point was strongly made by the President's Committee to Appraise Employment and Unemployment Statistics when it reported to President Kennedy in 1962.[8] But the reasons for breaking down the unemployment total go far beyond those implied in the preceding paragraph. It is the primary argument of this study that the United States does not really have a full-fledged employment policy if the employment goal is merely expressed in terms of the overall rate of unemployment. Table 1.2 suggests why this is so. It also points up dramatically how far we have been from anything that could reasonably be called a "full," "maximum," or even "satisfactory" employment situation.

Let us look at the three sets of paired columns in Table 1.2. Table 1.1 shows us that the national unemployment rate in 1965 was 4.6 per cent. But for married men, the rate was only 2.4 per cent. Is this a satisfactorily low rate because it is consider-

TABLE 1.1. Selected Measures of Unemployment in the United States, 1947-1965
(per cent)

Year	Unemployment Rate		Percentage of Labor Force Time Lost[b]
	Civilian Labor Force	Adult Males[a]	
1947	3.9	---	---
1948	3.8	3.2	---
1949	5.9	5.4	---
1950	5.3	4.7	---
1951	3.3	2.5	---
1952	3.1	2.4	---
1953	2.9	2.5	---
1954	5.6	4.9	---
1955	4.4	3.8	---
1956	4.2	3.4	5.1
1957	4.3	3.6	5.3
1958	6.8	6.2	8.1
1959	5.5	4.7	6.6
1960	5.6	4.7	6.7
1961	6.7	5.7	8.0
1962	5.6	4.6	6.7
1963	5.7	4.5	6.4[c]
1964	5.2	3.9	5.8
1965	4.6	3.2	5.0

Source: Manpower Report of the President, March 1966, and Employment and Earnings and Monthly Report on the Labor Force, February 1966.

[a] Aged 20 and over.

[b] Includes total unemployment and involuntary part-time unemployment.

[c] Beginning in 1963 this series was revised to reflect whether unemployed persons sought full- or part-time work. On the basis of the earlier definition the figure for this year would have been 6.8.

TABLE 1.2. Unemployment Rates for Selected Sectors of the Labor Force, 1950-1965
(Unemployed as percentage of civilian labor force in each group)

Year	Age 14-19, Both Sexes	Married Men	Professional-Technical	Laborers	White	Nonwhite
1950	11.3		2.2	11.7	4.9	9.1
1951	7.7		1.5	5.6	3.1	5.3
1952	8.0		1.0	5.7	2.8	5.4
1953	7.1		.9	6.1	2.7	4.5
1954	11.4		1.6	10.7	5.0	9.8
1955	10.2	2.8	1.0	10.2	3.9	8.7
1956	10.4	2.6	1.0	8.2	3.7	8.4
1957	10.8	2.8	1.2	9.4	3.9	8.0
1958	14.4	5.1	2.0	14.9	6.1	12.6
1959	13.2	3.6	1.7	12.4	4.9	10.7
1960	13.6	3.7	1.7	12.5	5.0	10.2
1961	15.2	4.6	2.0	14.5	6.0	12.5
1962	13.3	3.6	1.7	12.4	4.9	11.0
1963	15.6	3.4	1.8	12.1	5.1	10.9
1964	14.7	2.8	1.7	10.6	4.6	9.8
1965	13.6	2.4	1.5	8.4	4.1	8.3

Source: Employment and Earnings and Monthly Report on the Labor Force, February 1966, and Manpower Report of the President, March 1966.

ably less than 4 per cent? The unemployment rate for this group had fallen below 2 per cent in the first half of 1966 (when the overall rate averaged about 3.9 per cent).[9]

Now let us investigate the teen-agers. Obviously, it is too much to expect to bring the rate for this group down to 4 per cent.[10] But what is a reasonable "full employment" equivalent for teen-agers? Should we seek to hold unemployment for this group down to a rate equivalent to one-and-a-half, or two, or two-and-a-half times the national rate? The teen-age unemployment rate has worsened relative to the national rate during the 1960's, and in 1965 it was about three times the latter.[11] The comparable ratio in 1957 was only about 2.5 to 1. It can be fairly said that the high unemployment rates among youth in recent years represent a double failure of our employment policy. The overall unemployment rate has been at an unsatisfactorily

high level; and we have failed to reduce the large multiple that
the teen-age percentage bears to the national figure. These two
failures together have kept the teen-age unemployment rate consistently above 10 per cent since the end of the Korean War.
From 1958 through 1965 the teen-age rate remained above 13
per cent.

The second pair of columns in Table 1.2 presents an even
more striking contrast. The unemployment rate among unskilled
laborers tends to be some six to eight times that for the skilled
professional-technical group. (Interestingly, and contrary to general impressions, this relative gap has not widened since the
mid-fifties.)[12] Can we say that unemployment among professional-technical workers in 1965 was at a satisfactorily low level
because it was as low as 1.5 per cent? The rate was even lower
in 1956–1957.

The very low rates for these highly skilled workers suggest
another aspect of employment policy that we have not yet mentioned. A full-fledged employment policy must be concerned with
adjusting supply to demand as well as demand to supply. If
vacancies exceed, or are expected soon to exceed, the available
supply of workers of a particular type, then a full-fledged employment policy would involve measures to increase the supply
of these particular types of labor. Perhaps too simple a way
of expressing this is to state that employment policy must be
concerned with unemployment rates that are too low as well
as with those that are too high.

Let us turn back to Table 1.2 and to the story it tells about
the job market for unskilled laborers. Here again, as in the
teen-age situation we have a double default in our employment
policy. Not only has unemployment been unsatisfactorily high
for the labor force as a whole over most of the postwar period,
but we have also made little progress in reducing what we may
call the "structural differential" that makes the unemployment
rate for this group about twice the national rate.[13]

Having made our point, we need not linger long over the familiar contrast between white and nonwhite unemployment rates.
Even if he had succeeded in consistently keeping total unemployment down to about 4 per cent of the labor force in recent
years, the rate for nonwhites would have been in the neighbor-

hood of 8 per cent. This could hardly be said to reflect a "full," "maximum," or even "satisfactory" level of employment for this substantial segment of the American population.

Let us now refer for a moment to the last column of Table 1.1. These figures suggest yet another dimension with which a national employment policy must be concerned. A person may be partially rather than wholly unemployed, and the last column of Table 1.1 provides estimates of total time lost through involuntary part-time employment as well as through total unemployment. If we think of 4 per cent as a satisfactorily low unemployment rate, is this rate to cover only the wholly unemployed? If it is to cover part-time unemployment as well, then our overall record in the last decade has been worse than the first column of Table 1.1 suggests.

There is still another respect in which the figures in Table 1.1 underestimate the extent of involuntary unemployment. If, in a poor job market, a man or woman finally gives up looking for work because none seems to be available, he or she is dropped from the official count of the unemployed. Such people are said to have withdrawn from the labor force. While in a very real sense they are still unemployed, their unemployment is said to be "disguised." The important thing is that they are no longer officially counted as unemployed although they still want jobs and would go to work if suitable employment were offered them.[14]

It is virtually impossible to obtain reliable estimates of such disguised unemployment, but we do know that it varies with the amount of recorded unemployment.[15] Is our goal for a satisfactory unemployment rate—whether 4 per cent or some other figure—to include this "disguised unemployment"? It seems clear that at least some of it should be included. To the extent that we do include it, the figures in Table 1.1 further understate the failure of American employment policy in recent years.

The Contrast with Europe

This failure stands out in glaring contrast to the record of the advanced economies of Western Europe in recent years.

Table 1.3 puts this contrast into sharp focus. If, for the moment, we take these figures at their face value, we see that not a single one of the European countries listed had an unemployment rate as high as 4 per cent between 1961 and 1964. Of the countries listed, only Italy has experienced unemployment significantly in excess of 4 per cent since 1955; and over this same period, only Italy again has had an unemployment rate higher than that in the United States in some years (all before 1960). In the last six years or more shown in Table 1.3, France, West Germany, The Netherlands, Sweden, and the United Kingdom were regularly operating at unemployment rates well below 3 per cent, and usually below 2 per cent. Labor shortage, not exces-

TABLE 1.3. Per cent of Civilian Labor Force Unemployed in Selected European Countries and the United States, 1950-1964

Year	Belgium	France	Germany[c] (Fed. Rep.)	Italy	Netherlands	Sweden	United[d] Kingdom	United States
1950	5.0		7.2		2.1	2.2	1.2	5.3
1951	4.4		6.4		2.5	1.8	0.9	3.3
1952	5.2		6.1		3.6	2.3	1.5	3.1
1953	5.5		5.5		2.6	2.8	1.3	2.9
1954	5.2	1.7	5.2	8.2	1.9	2.6	1.0	5.6
1955	4.0	1.5	3.9	7.1	1.3	2.5	0.9	4.4
1956	2.9	1.1	3.1	8.9	0.9	1.7	0.9	4.2
1957	2.4	0.9	2.7	7.1	1.2	1.9	1.1	4.3
1958	3.4	0.9	2.7	6.1	2.4	2.5	1.6	6.8
1959	4.0	1.4 (2.8)	1.9 (1.6)	5.3 (5.7)	1.9	2.0[a]	1.7 (3.1)	5.5
1960[b]	3.4	1.3 (2.7)	1.0 (0.7)	4.0 (4.3)	1.1	1.8[a]	1.3 (2.4)	5.6
1961[b]	2.7	1.1 (2.4)	0.7 (0.4)	3.5 (3.7)	0.8	1.5 (1.5)	1.1 (2.3)	6.7
1962[b]	2.2	1.3 (2.5)	0.6 (0.4)	3.0 (3.2)	0.7	1.5 (1.5)	1.6 (2.9)	5.6
1963[b]	1.9	1.3 (3.1)	0.7 (0.5)	2.4 (2.7)	0.7	1.7 (1.7)	1.9 (3.4)	5.7
1964[b]	1.5	1.1 (2.5)	0.6 (0.4)	2.8 (2.9)	0.7	1.6 (1.6)	1.4 (2.5)	5.2

Source: Manpower Statistics, 1950-1962 (Paris: Organization for Economic Co-operation and Development, 1963) and Manpower Statistics, 1954-1964 (Paris: OECD, 1965) except for the American figures and the Swedish data for 1950 to 1959. The latter are from International Labor Review, Statistical Supplement, LXX (November 1954), 98, and Yearbook of Labour Statistics, 1962 (Geneva: International Labour Office, 1962), Table 10. Minor changes in the method of compiling the Swedish data occurred in 1956 and 1960. American data are from Manpower Report of the President, March, 1966.

[a]Revised figures not available.
[b]The figures in parentheses for these years are unemployment rates revised to correspond to American definitions. They are taken from A. F. Neef, "International Unemployment Rates, 1960-64," Monthly Labor Review, LXXXVIII (March 1965), 258. Figures for 1964 are preliminary.
[c]Includes West Berlin from 1960 on, but not before.
[d]The figures revised to American definitions for 1959-1964 are for Great Britain only.

sive unemployment, was the chief problem. (Unemployment did increase significantly in some of these countries in 1965–1966.)

However, we need to ask at this point, are these figures actually comparable with the American estimates? Is unemployment defined in the same way, and are comparable statistical procedures used in all of these countries? The figures in parentheses for 1959–1964 in Table 1.3 provide a partial answer to this question. These figures provide revised unemployment rates adjusted to correspond to American definitions. The revisions were made by the United States Bureau of Labor Statistics.[16] Unfortunately, similar revised figures are not available for earlier years.

The adjustments effected by the figures in parentheses are modest, being largest for France and England. By and large, what we said previously about low unemployment in Europe still holds. Unemployment rates of 3 per cent or less (frequently much less) have been the rule in recent years. A number of European countries have had serious unemployment problems at some time during the last fifteen years. We can mention the absorption of refugees in West Germany, some difficult problems of adjustment in Belgium, and the continuing struggle with unemployment and underemployment in Italy's Mezzogiorno. But despite this, unemployment rates as high as 3 per cent by American definitions have been the exception rather than the rule in recent years.

This is not to imply that it is reasonable to assume that "full employment" in the United States corresponds to as low an unemployment rate as does full employment in these European countries. This is a problem to which we shall give some attention in a later chapter. In general, the European countries listed in Table 1.3 assume that full employment corresponds to an unemployment rate in the neighborhood of 2 per cent—perhaps in a range of from less than 2 per cent to somewhat less than 3 per cent by American definitions, depending on the country. On the whole, the full employment goal has been set at a high level, and even at this high level the goal in recent years has been much more consistently achieved (or surpassed) than in the United States.

Indeed, a double contrast must be made between Europe and the United States in the matter of employment goals. The first contrast is in the record of achievement that we have just described; the other is in the level and direction of aspirations. Almost without exception, the European democracies have raised their sights with respect to the employment objective over the last decade. Rates of unemployment that were considered satisfactory a decade or more ago are now considered to be unacceptably high. Sights have been raised as to how much unemployment is consistent with full employment. One can say that a "ratchet effect" has been at work. The longer unemployment remains at levels of 3 or 2 per cent or less, the stronger has become the resolve not to permit a return to unemployment levels of 4 or 5 per cent (or more) that once were considered satisfactory or at least acceptable.[17]

In contrast, until the success of the tax cut in 1964 became apparent to virtually everyone, it almost appeared that American sights with respect to the goal of full employment had been lowered somewhat.[18] It is true that the magic number of 4 per cent continued to be widely quoted, and beginning in 1961 the Council of Economic Advisers espoused the 4 per cent figure as only a first step, toward a still lower unemployment rate. However, as is brought out in Table 1.1, the unemployment rate remained above 5 per cent through 1964 and still averaged 4.6 per cent in 1965. Until very recently, it appeared that Congress and the American people were prepared to live indefinitely with unemployment of more than 4 per cent—and that other economic goals, particularly price stability and equilibrium in the balance of payments at the present gold value of the dollar, were given precedence over full employment defined as 4 per cent or less of the labor force.

The success of the tax cut in 1964 and the wider acceptance, in Congress and in the country at large, of the "New Economics" have certainly changed matters to some extent. Equally important, there has been a growing sensitivity in the United States to the tragically high unemployment rates among Negroes, youth, and the unskilled and least educated generally. With this growing sensitivity has gone increased appreciation of the fact that reduction of these differentially high unemployment rates requires not only selective measures of manpower policy— which have expanded rapidly since 1961—but also the kind of monetary-fiscal policy that, by raising aggregate demand, will bring down the overall unemployment rate to 4 per cent or even lower.

While it is fair to say, then, that we have raised our sights with respect to the employment goal in the last two or three years, we must also remember that it required the extra stimulus provided by the intensification of our military effort in South Vietnam to bring the unemployment rate down to 4 per cent and less in 1966. It remains to be seen, if and when defense expenditures are reduced, how far Americans are prepared to go in insisting on government action that will keep total unemployment at 4 per cent or less of the labor force.

Increasing public insistence on a strict interpretation of the full employment objective is a political fact of life that European governments know they cannot ignore. Until very recently, this has not been true in the United States. In view of what has been learned in the last few years, it is not likely that American public opinion will again accept seven consecutive years of more than 5 per cent unemployment. But it remains to be seen how high an employment standard Americans will insist on under more or less normal peacetime conditions, when national defense does not provide the same justification for a large increase in government expenditures as was present in 1965–1966.

The Issues Involved

Why has the United States failed to achieve a reasonable approximation of full employment during so much of the last decade? Attempts to answer this question must deal with at least three sets of interrelated issues.[19]

First, the implementation of full employment policy was impeded by uncertainty as to the underlying causes of the high level of unemployment after 1957. How much of the unemployment was due to structural changes which made an increasing fraction of the labor force unsuited for the jobs that were available? And how much was due to a deficiency of aggregate demand—to a failure of total spending (on goods and services) to increase at the rate required for full employment of a growing and increasingly productive labor force? The policies that are appropriate hinge on the answers that we give to these questions.

The answers that have, in fact, been given often reflect a second set of issues—the priorities that different groups attach to full employment and to the other economic goals with which it might possibly conflict. The most important of these potentially competitive policy goals are price stability and balance-of-payments equilibrium at fixed exchange rates.

It is not unfair to say that a good deal of the insistence in some quarters on the "structural" character of unemployment stems not so much from intensive analysis of underlying causes but from fear that the alternative diagnosis would lead to action, in the form of enlarged government deficits and easier monetary policy, that would accelerate the rise in wages and prices and cause further deterioration in the balance of payments.[20] The potential conflict between full employment and other policy goals is the subject of Chapter 2.

This brings us to the third set of issues which underlies the American failure to maintain a successful employment policy. Prevailing public opinion—as reflected in the press, in the halls of Congress, and in the business community—has revealed an interrelated set of fears: fear of a growing public debt resulting from continued federal deficits and fear of continued government encroachment on private economic activity. The American concern over budgetary deficits and the government debt has no counterpart in Europe, even in business circles.[21] Nor does the broad range of public opinion in Europe reveal the same fear of "big government" that is reflected across a broad spectrum of public opinion in the United States.[22]

American experience, at least until 1964, suggests that we might state the problem in this way. When the unemployment rate was in the range of 5 to 6 per cent, social evaluations as reflected in the political process were such as to give more weight to the fear of fiscal irresponsibility and increased government intervention than to the desirability of further reduction in the unemployment rate. The difficulties which the Kennedy and Johnson Administrations faced in pushing through the tax reduction that was finally approved in early 1964 illustrates the deep-seated concern in influential circles over the issue of "fiscal responsibility." And the fact that the stimulus took the form of tax reduction rather than increased government expenditures reflected the more deeply seated fear of the power inherent in big government.[23]

As already noted, the success of the tax cut in 1964 has brought wider acceptance of the New Economics and a greater willingness to use an expansionary fiscal policy to reduce unemployment. But the fear of "big government" and of rising nondefense expenditures by the federal government still remains. Under Lyndon Johnson, this fear has perhaps been tempered somewhat by aspirations directed toward the Great Society and growing sensitivity to the need to create employment opportunities for the underprivileged. Almost certainly, Congress and the American people place a somewhat stricter interpretation on the goal of full employment today than they did at the beginning of the 1960's, although they have not yet moved as far in this direction as have the industrial nations of Western Europe.

Let us now examine more carefully the ways of reconciling the full employment objective with other goals of economic policy in the European democracies and in the United States. This is our task in Chapters 2 and 3.

NOTES

1. Herbert Stein and E. F. Denison, "High Employment and Growth in the American Economy," in *Goals for Americans*, Report of the President's Commission on National Goals (Englewood Cliffs, New Jersey: Prentice-Hall, 1960), p. 164.

2. My italics.

3. *Goals for Americans*, p. 10.

4. From "Some Reflections on the Employment Act," an address delivered at the Annual Meeting of the American Statistical Association, Minneapolis, Minnesota, September 7, 1962.

5. *Employment Act of 1946*, Sec. 1.

6. *Goals for Americans*, p. 10. An "ultimate" goal for the United States of an unemployment rate of about 3 per cent has considerable support. This matter of what numbers to use in defining full employment is discussed at some length in Chapter 3. Our own recommendations are presented in Chapter 7.

7. Canada has had a similar experience, with unemployment rates above 5 per cent from 1958 through 1963.

8. *Measuring Employment and Unemployment* (Washington: Government Printing Office, 1962), p. 42.

9. These figures for the first half of 1966 are seasonally adjusted.

10. The problem of teen-age unemployment is treated at some length in Chapter 6.

11. This worsening became noticeable in 1963. See the discussion of teen-age unemployment in Chapter 6.

12. See Chapter 6.

13. In 1965 the rate for laborers fell below twice the national rate for the first time since 1951. (For the period before 1957, the comparison is based on pre-1957 definitions.)

14. For further discussion of such disguised unemployment and for references to some of the relevant literature, see Chapter 3.

15. One recent study estimated that inclusion of disguised unemployment would have raised the unemployment rate in 1962 from 5.6 to 8.5 per cent. See T. F. Dernburg and K. T. Strand, "Hidden Unemployment, 1953–62: A Quantitative Analysis by Age and Sex," *American Economic Review,* **LVI** (March 1966), 94. The Clark Subcommittee ventured the guess that in 1964 disguised unemployment amounted to somewhere between 800,000 and 1,500,000 persons. Even the lower end of this range would have added about 20 per cent to the official unemployment rate of 5.2 per cent in 1964. See Subcommittee on Employment and Manpower of the Senate Committee on Labor and Public Welfare, *Toward Full Employment: Proposals for a Comprehensive Employment and Manpower Policy in the United States* (Washington: Government Printing Office, 1964), p. 32.

16. The estimates for 1960 were first published in the report of the President's Committee to Appraise Employment and Unemployment Statistics, *Measuring Employment and Unemployment,* Chapter X and Appendix A. Revised estimates for 1960–1964 are presented by A. F. Neef, "International Unemployment Rates, 1960–1964," *Monthly Labor Review,* **LXXXVIII** (March 1965), 256–259. It should be noted that some modest standardization of the official figures for the various European countries had already been attempted by OECD in putting together the figures in Table 1.3.

17. "Nearly everywhere in the region [Western Europe] a profound attitudinal change appears to have taken place over the past several decades with respect to the responsibilities of governments in economic affairs. To put the matter perhaps too simply, modern governments in the democracies of Western Europe appear much more fearful of the prospect of unemployment than of inflation." J. F. Dewhurst et al., *Europe's Needs and Resources* (New York: Twentieth Century Fund, 1961), p. 28. This is still a valid statement even when we take account of the efforts from time to time by some countries—for example, the United Kingdom in 1966—to curb inflation by means that temporarily increase unemployment.

18. Thus one Congressman was moved to say in 1964 that: "We have been successively lowering our sights on how much unemployment is

too much." Henry S. Reuss, *The Critical Decade* (New York: McGraw-Hill, 1964), p. 159. The same view was expressed at about the same time by Arthur M. Ross: "During the recent period of economic slack, there has been a tendency to relax the criteria [as to how much unemployment is consistent with full employment]." Arthur M. Ross (ed.), *Unemployment and the American Economy* (New York: John Wiley and Sons, 1964), p. 19. Or, to quote a British observer, the late Jack Downie, we have "the contrast between the political cash value which full employment has had in most European countries and the political tolerance for unemployment which has existed, and still exists, in the United States." See his paper in Ross (ed.), *op. cit.,* p. 161.

19. For useful background on the questions raised in this section, see Ross (ed.), *loc. cit.*

20. "The structural school of thought, too, has its hyperenthusiasts. These are not labor economists, but fiscal conservatives, who as an alternative to expansionary policies argue that a job is available for every unemployed person if only he had the requisite skill or would move to the appropriate locale. . . . Advocacy of the structural explanation does not necessarily entail support of structural legislation among this group." Subcommittee on Employment and Manpower, *op. cit.,* p. 28.

21. As Angus Maddison has put it: "The U.S. emphasis on the virtues of a balanced budget has had no post-war counterpart in Europe, where there are no statutory limits on fiscal policy such as the ceiling on government debt and on the interest rates payable on longer-term government securities as in the United States. The constitutional system of checks and balances in the United States makes it more difficult for an administration to change taxes quickly than is the case in Europe." *Economic Growth in the West* (London: Allen and Unwin, 1964), p. 117.

22. These fears of deficit spending, government debt, and "big government" are part of the "American Business Creed," a creed which is held in varying degrees by a substantial segment of middle-class public opinion in the United States. See F. X. Sutton et al., *The American Business Creed* (Cambridge, Mass.: Harvard University Press, 1956; paperback edition, 1962). It is worth noting the comment of these authors (p. 373) that: "To a remarkable degree the creed's opposition to government centers on government deficits and debt." See also Sidney Alexander, "Opposition to Deficit Spending for the Prevention of Unemployment," in *Income, Employment and Public Policy: Essays in Honor of Alvin H. Hansen* (New York: Norton, 1948), pp. 177–198.

23. The following statements by former President Eisenhower preceding the 1964 presidential election campaign are worth quoting in this connection:

"We are headed *away* from known-sound fiscal policies and balanced budgets . . . *toward* experimental and highly dangerous federal overspending which inevitably leads to inflation, deterioration of our currency and loss of world confidence in the dollar.

"It must be emphasized that a tax cut alone is only half of the equation.

Without a commensurate curtailment of federal expenditures a tax reduction by itself is a cruel illusion: what is given to the taxpayer in one hand is more than taken away from the other by cheapening his money and increasing his burden of public debt."

Both paragraphs are from "Why I am a Republican," *Saturday Evening Post*, April 11, 1964, pp. 18, 19. Italics were in the original. In view of the title of the article, it should be added that a substantial number of Democrats share these views.

CHAPTER 2

The Aggregative Goals of Economic Policy

Full employment is only one of a battery of "aggregative economic goals" which today are espoused, more or less explicitly, in both Western Europe and the United States. The goals are interrelated, and the same instruments of monetary-fiscal policy can be used, in varying degrees, to pursue them. How full employment is defined and what is done to achieve it depend in good part upon what is done about the other aggregative goals.

The List of Goals

In addition to full employment, the aggregative goals usually cited are: rapid economic growth, price stability, and balance-of-payments equilibrium. To these we can add something that has come to be called "incomes policy." The goal in the last case is to hold the expansion in total money income to the rise in total output. Since wages loom so large in total income, this goal amounts to that of restricting the relative rise in average money wages to the rate of increase in average labor productivity, supplemented by some restraint on the increase in total nonwage income. We shall have more to say about all of these goals as the discussion develops.

There are, of course, many other economic goals with which governments are concerned—satisfying collective needs for education, defense, and the like; improving the distribution of income and wealth among individuals and groups; promoting the interests of particular regions or sectors of the economy; conserving natural resources; and so on.[1] But our five aggregative goals stand in a class by themselves. They are concerned with crucial economic aggregates: total employment, total output, the general level of prices, the total of payments to and receipts from the rest of the world, and total money incomes. These aggregative variables are all interrelated. And they are all subject to some degree of control through the two main types of aggregative economic policy—fiscal policy (the management of the government's tax receipts and expenditures) and monetary policy.[2]

Obviously, we cannot discuss full employment as a policy goal without considering these other aggregative goals. The variables on which these goals depend are all interrelated. Pursuit of the employment goal is almost certain to affect in greater or less degree the rate of growth, the level of money incomes, the general level of prices, and the balance of payments. Our aggregative goals are thus to some degree interdependent. It remains to be seen to what degree these goals are complementary and to what degree competitive.

Differences in Priorities

The priorities attached to these aggregative goals will not be the same for all governments and will also vary among individuals and groups in any one country. Differences in priorities may arise from two sources. First, value judgments may vary, and second, disagreement may exist as to the relevant underlying economic relationships. These two sets of differences are not unrelated.

Let us consider first the matter of value judgments, a subject which always leaves the professional economist ill at ease. To one individual or group, a decline of one-half of 1 per cent in the national unemployment rate, when the latter is at 5 per cent, may seem to entail a much larger gain in "social welfare" than, say, a deceleration in the rise in the consumers' price index from 3 per cent last year to 2 per cent this year. Another group's social priorities may lead to just the opposite conclusion.

The other reason why these aggregative goals may be ordered differently by various groups involves the uncertainty and disagreement that may exist concerning underlying relationships. Thus, a vigorous debate still goes on as to the relationship between the level of unemployment, on the one hand, and the rate of change in prices (and wages), on the other.[3] Another illustration can be drawn from recent American experience.

Those who have favored an expansionary monetary-fiscal policy to reduce unemployment and stimulate growth have been inclined to argue that such an expansionary policy would not necessarily lead to a serious worsening in the American balance of payments. For one thing, it was thought that accelerated domestic expansion might significantly reduce the flow of private capital from the United States to the rest of the world. (This has not, in fact, turned out to be the case.) It was also argued that faster growth would mean accelerated increases in labor productivity and thereby improvement in the competitive position of at least some of our export industries.[4]

The opposing group, those who have argued that aggressive pursuit of the full employment goal would seriously worsen the balance-of-payments situation, have maintained that expansion of aggregate demand would increase imports while worsening the competitive position of American exports. Hence the accelerated rise in aggregate demand would cause an accelerated rise in imports; and, at the same time, the expansion in domestic demand would push up costs and prices relative to prices abroad and thus lead to a decline, or at least to a marked retardation in the growth, of American exports.

Thus the relative priorities attached to the different aggregative goals tend to vary—among countries, among groups within a country, and within a country over a period of years. As we have already noted, the employment goal today is given a higher relative priority on both sides of the Atlantic than it ever had been given before the onset of the Great Depression. And the goal of rapid economic growth is emphasized much more today, particularly in Western Europe, than it was a generation ago.

Within any one country, as we should expect, the ordering of our five goals varies as we move across the political spectrum. To the left of center, primary emphasis is placed on full employment and rapid growth. As we move to the right of the spectrum, top priority comes to be attached to price (and wage) stability and balance-of-payments equilibrium.[5]

In the broad middle spectrum of political opinion in the United States, the priority attached to a fairly strict interpretation of the employment goal is clearly lower than it is in the comparable middle spectrum of opinion in any of the Western European democracies. Full employment and rapid growth carry higher priorities in Europe than in the United States. Conversely, price stability has carried a higher priority in the United States. As one thoughtful observer has put it:

> It is always unwise to shun the obvious. And the most obvious explanation, which fits not only the facts but also what people have said, is quite simply that Americans weakly chose employment because they chose price stability strongly. It may be that "price stability" has often been used as a convenient shorthand for "sound economic policies" . . . . But it is hard to avoid the conclusion that the contrast between European and American price history from 1956 to 1962 is an accurate index of a contrast in attitudes. Much has been said in Europe about the importance of price stability. But nowhere—not even in Germany, supposedly the classic example of inflation neurosis—have countries been prepared in the event to arrest their growth and create unemployment simply in order to stop prices from rising.[6]

This was written in 1963. The contrast still exists, although, as we indicated in Chapter 1, it is perhaps not as marked today as it was in the early 1960's.

The Target Variables and Economic Welfare

We must now ask: What are the "target variables" in terms of which success in achieving our aggregative goals is to be measured?[7] When we espouse these aggregative goals, to what specific economic variables is our attention addressed?

We have already seen what the key target variable is in the case of employment policy. It is the rate of unemployment—the fraction of the labor force unemployed. And the goal of full employment can be described as the objective of keeping the national unemployment rate at or below some level—say, 3 or 4 per cent in the United States.[8]

What target variables are implied by our other aggregative goals?

Economic growth refers to the output of goods and services and is most conveniently measured in terms of the gross national product (GNP) in constant prices. The growth goal is usually expressed in terms of a desired average percentage increase in real GNP per year over some period.[9]

The target variable for price stability is usually considered to be some comprehensive price index—ordinarily either the official consumers' price index or the comprehensive price index applicable to the entire GNP. The objective is to hold the percentage rate of change per period in this price index to some maximum—say, a rise of not more than 1 or 2 per cent per year.

What target variable do we have in mind when we mention the need to maintain balance-of-payments equilibrium? The intent is to prevent an embarrassing decline in a country's international monetary reserves, which usually consist of gold and net holdings of liquid assets denominated in the leading convertible currencies of other countries. Balance-of-payments equilibrium therefore implies no persistent decline in a country's international monetary reserves or, possibly, a steady, moderate increase in such reserves in line with the growth of the country's total transactions with the rest of the world.

Now we consider incomes policy. Essentially, the goal here is to restrain the rise in total money income to the increase in total output. As we noted earlier in this chapter, this goal typically takes the form of holding the rise in money wages to the increase in labor productivity. Our target variable here can thus be expressed in one of several ways. The usual way is in terms of average money wages per worker per year, and the goal is to restrict the rise in this variable to the increase in output per manyear.

When a government espouses our five aggregative goals, we may assume that the policy makers have in mind some crude notion of a "social welfare function" which expresses the way in which the national welfare, as they conceive it, depends on the behavior of the target variables that we have just described. Thus, ordinarily, welfare will be thought to increase if unemployment falls or the rate of growth accelerates and to decline if the price level rises at an accelerated rate. In the economist's terms, the policy maker seeks to make social welfare (as he views it) as large as possible by bringing about changes in the target variables. To change the target variables, he uses the policy instruments at his disposal—here, chiefly, the instruments of fiscal and monetary policy.[10]

In practice, of course, this process of maximizing social welfare is only very crudely approximated. Thus, when targets are set, such as an unemployment rate of 4 per cent, a growth rate of 5 per cent, and so on, these targets represent abbreviations of rough notions regarding the way in which social welfare is assumed to vary with changes in the unemployment rate, the growth rate, and the other target variables.[11]

Before we proceed further to look at the way in which social welfare is related to our aggregative target variables, a statement should be made about the use of the phrase "social welfare" in these pages. Economic theory has long—and fruitlessly— struggled to derive scientific propositions about the relations between social well-being and the traditional economic variables that are independent of personal value judgments.[12] We have nothing to contribute to this literature. But, as numerous writers have pointed out, economists have nothing to say about questions of economic policy unless they concern themselves with possible changes in economic welfare; and to do so requires the application of value judgments, either one's own or those of someone else. "If the economist feels incompetent to make such [value judgments] himself, he should at least admit their legitimacy and provide the analytical framework to help others to make these judgments."[13]

In this book, we shall permit value judgments and notions of economic welfare to enter in two ways. For the remainder of this chapter, we shall accept the notions of economic welfare that are implied by attempts to achieve various combinations of values for our five target variables. We take as given the sets of values that lead to more or less emphasis being placed on low unemployment, stability of prices, rapid growth, and so on. We are concerned only with exploring some of the economic implications of the policy targets that are adopted (or advocated) and of seeking to clarify the way in which economic welfare, defined in a particular way, is affected by the behavior of these target variables.[14]

Later on, particularly in Chapter 7, but also to some extent in Chapters 3 and 4, we shall introduce value judgments of our own, which others are, of course, free to accept or reject as they please. This is inevitable if we are to make recommendations as to what we consider to be a desirable set of employment goals for the United States. And that is the most important purpose of this book.

An Aggregative Welfare Function

Let us now return to our social welfare function and to the target variables that we derived from the aggregative policy goals. When these aggregative goals are espoused, it is implied that national economic welfare (Z) is related in some way to the following variables or constraints:

1. The rate of overall unemployment u.
2. The rate of growth in total output $\dot{Y}$.
3. The rate of change in a country's international monetary reserves $\dot{A}$. This is one measure of the degree to which "balance-of-payments equilibrium" is achieved.
4. The rate of change in the general price level $\dot{P}$.
5. And some measure of wage restraint, for which we might write $\dot{W} - \dot{y}$, or the difference between the rate of change in wages per manyear and in productivity per manyear.

All the rates of change listed here are to be taken in percentage terms.

Now let us see how current debate and policy action suggest that total economic welfare is considered to be related to these variables or constraints. However, for reasons that will become clear in a moment, we must first introduce the following two additional elements:

6. Let n represent some notion of the rate of increase in the domestic price level beyond which the functioning of the domestic economy (apart from balance-of-payments considerations) becomes impaired because of "loss of confidence in the currency."

7. Let us also add two additional price variables: P_d, or an index of domestic prices of goods that move in international trade, and P_f, to represent an index of foreign prices of the same goods.

The pursuit of our five aggregative goals can now be described as follows:

$$Z = f(u, \dot{Y}, \dot{P})$$

subject to the following constraints:

$$\dot{A} = k \pm e$$
$$\dot{P}_d - \dot{P}_f \leqslant m \pm f$$
$$\dot{W} - \dot{y} \leqslant \dot{P}_f + m \pm g$$
$$\dot{P} \leqslant n$$
$$u \leqslant q$$

where $e, f, g, k, m, n,$ and q are constants.

Let us consider first the expression in parentheses. This states that economic welfare changes in some way with changes in the three variables inside the parentheses.[15] These variables relate to only three of our aggregative goals: employment, growth, and price stability. The other two goals are listed as constraints, and prices and unemployment appear again as constraints as well as variables within the parentheses.

The significance of the distinction between what is inside the parentheses of the Z function and what are listed as constraints can be expressed as follows. The variables in parentheses can vary over some range; and, given the policy maker's rough notions about the nature of the function, he can try roughly to maximize welfare by seeking to change the values for these "target variables."[16] His freedom to do so is limited by the constraints. These play a negative or restraining role. The policy maker is not free to vary these elements to any significant degree as he seeks to increase social welfare.

This way of viewing macroeconomic policy permits us to differentiate among our aggregative goals. One can say that employment and growth are positive goals. Both can vary over some range, and economic policy can seek to change them so as to increase economic welfare as viewed by the policy maker. Welfare will be increased as the unemployment rate is reduced and as the rate of growth of output is accelerated. Welfare is also related to the rate of change in prices, but in a complex way—and the nature of this relationship throws some light on the different ways in which the employment and growth goals have been pursued in various European countries and the United States.

First, virtually all governments and the vast majority of their citizens place some positive value on a stable price level, and a movement in the price level either upward or downward presumably detracts from welfare as viewed by the policy maker. However, I do not think that this relationship, taken by itself, is as strong as is generally assumed. Within a moderate range, variation in the price level *in and of itself* is not considered to have a strong effect on economic welfare. (This statement is less true of Germany and the United States than of most other countries.) Price stability is important, but it is important chiefly as a *constraint*—and as a constraint at two different levels. To understand this, we must look at the entire set of constraints listed in connection with our welfare function, beginning with that for the balance of payments.[17]

Aggregative Goals as Constraints: The Balance of Payments

We expressed the balance-of-payments constraint as

$$\dot{A} = k \pm e$$

This states the condition that the percentage change in international monetary reserves should be equal to k plus or minus a margin or error e. The value of k might be zero. In this case, no change in the stock of monetary reserves is desired, and any change in excess of e requires compensatory action.

In terms of our social welfare function, what does it mean to state that the balance-of-payments objective should be viewed as a constraint? For simplicity, let us take just two of our other goals—employment and growth—and write the welfare function

$$Z = f(u, \dot{Y})$$

subject to the constraint that $\dot{A}$ should not be less than zero or greater than some amount e. That is,

$$0 \leqslant \dot{A} \leqslant e$$

Let us assume now that the constraint is in danger of being violated through disequilibrium in the balance of payments. The overriding need to stay within the limits of the constraint means that u and $\dot{Y}$ cease to provide the same guide to policy as before. Steps will be taken to preserve or restore equilibrium even if the needed action has an effect on unemployment and growth that, taken by itself, would reduce welfare.

Paradoxically, one or more of the variables inside the parentheses of our welfare function may now themselves become constraints. Assume that the steps that would ordinarily be taken to reduce the external deficit would also bring about a substantial increase in unemployment. However, the policy maker's welfare function may imply an absolute ceiling on the unemployment rate. We have expressed this in our list of constraints as $u \leqslant q$, where q is the maximum rate of unemployment that would be tolerated. In more usual terms, it may be considered "politically impossible" to permit the unemployment rate to rise above, say, 5 per cent even for a short period, regardless of the consequences to the balance of payments. In this case the conflict of the two constraints would lead to unusual steps, depending on the circumstances—from emergency arrangements for international credits to, as a last resort, currency devaluation.

This is a fair approximation of the way these constraints have operated in Europe during the postwar period. Various European countries, particularly those to which foreign trade is especially important, have been forced from time to time to sacrifice some employment and growth because of the balance-of-payments constraint. However, they have been willing to do this only so long as the steps needed to restore external equilibrium did not force unemployment above what was considered politically tolerable. This upper limit on unemployment in Europe, after full allowance for differences in definition and measurement, has clearly been much lower than that in the United States.[18]

Recent American experience in dealing with the balance-of-payments constraint might be briefly summarized as follows.[19]

1. Because of the size of its gold holdings, the United States could afford to accept a negative value as a target goal for $\dot{A}$ for a number of years. But its willingness to do this has been declining *pari passu* with its gold stock. It now attaches a high priority to (a) continued success in reducing the rate of decline in A and (b) bringing the decline to a complete halt within a moderate period in the future.

2. Although the upper limit on the balance-of-payments deficit that the United States has been willing to accept has been, and still is, high by the standards of less affluent countries, American willingness to sacrifice employment and growth to stay within this limit has seemed high by European standards—and also by the standards of many economists. A number of economists have argued that in the first half of the 1960's the country was asked to pay too high a price, both in unemployment and in economic growth forgone, to stay within the balance-of-payments constraint.[20]

3. The counterpart of this criticism has taken the form of a variety of suggestions for restatement of the balance-of-payments constraint. These suggestions include devaluation to a lower goal content of the dollar, a floating exchange rate, and various proposals for reform of the international monetary system.[21]

4. The rapid expansion in aggregate demand and output after the 1964 tax cut did not bring with it the decline in private capital exports and resulting improvement in the balance of payments that some experts had predicted.[22] At the same time, although monetary policy was used to defend the balance of payments—particularly by pushing up short-term interest rates—the American authorities were not prepared, by restrictive measures,

to jeopardize the gratifying decline in unemployment that occurred during 1964–1965. Hence the effort was made to satisfy
the balance-of-payments constraint in ways that would permit
continued rapid expansion in output and employment and the
early achievement of the Administration's "interim" goal of full
employment (at an unemployment rate of 4 per cent). These
measures (some adopted before 1964) included the Interest
Equalization Tax on American purchases of foreign securities,
"tying" of foreign aid to exports from the United States, restraints on lending abroad by banks and other financial institu-
tions, similar restraints on investment abroad by large American
firms, efforts to stimulate exports and also to retard the rise
in tourist expenditures abroad, and improved and enlarged arrangements for international financial cooperation.

5. As the approach to full employment and to a full-capacity
level of output in 1965–1966 brought an accelerated rise in prices,
it became more feasible to use the conventional instruments of
monetary-fiscal policy to protect the balance of payments.
Efforts to restrain the rise in aggregate demand, when unemployment was at 4 per cent or below, involved significantly less
cost in terms of social welfare than they did when unemployment
was at 5 or 6 per cent; and, in addition, retardation of the
rise in prices was desired for its own sake as well as because
of its possible contribution to improvement in the balance of
payments.

Price Stability as a Constraint

Let us now examine the way in which price stability enters
into the policy maker's welfare function. The goal of price stability influences policy in three different ways, all of which are
represented in the symbols presented earlier.

1. Some positive value is attached to price stability for its
own sake. Hence we have included the rate of change in the
price level within the parenthetical expression of our welfare
function, the assumption being that welfare is inversely related
to the absolute rate of change in the price level.[23] Nevertheless,

I am prepared to argue that, in both Europe and the United States, the *independent* link between domestic price stability and social welfare, as the latter is viewed in the broad middle spectrum of public opinion, is not a terribly strong one. Within a significant range of price variation *and apart from the balance-of-payments problem*, no Western European government would be prepared to sacrifice any significant degree of employment or growth in order to reduce the rate of change in the price level.[24]

It is probably fair to say that more emphasis has been placed on the virtues of price stability in the United States than in most European countries.[25] But here the question can also be raised as to how much employment would be sacrificed for greater price stability, apart from balance-of-payments considerations. The emphasis on price stability in the United States in recent years, as in Europe, has been associated primarily with the balance-of-payments problem, and this relationship now occupies our attention.[26]

2. The second and most important way in which price stability influences policy is through its importance as an instrument to achieve balance-of-payments equilibrium. In serving in this capacity, price stability is not considered as making a positive, independent contribution to welfare in its own right. Instead, it is viewed as a constraint. Here, it is a constraint of the second order, which is required if the first-order constraint, balance-of-payments equilibrium, is to be maintained.

When we think of price stability in this role, the relevant target is not stability in the domestic price level, but some desired relationship between the domestic price level and that of the country's chief trading partners—between, to put it roughly, domestic and foreign price levels.[27]

Thus we formulated this constraint as having the form

$$\dot{P}_d - \dot{P}_f \leqslant m \pm f$$

That is, the difference between the rate of change in the domestic and foreign price levels should not exceed an amount m—plus or minus, in the short run, a margin of error f. Obviously this constraint does not require a stable price level. If $\dot{P}_f$ is rising rapidly, $\dot{P}_d$ may also rise rapidly. All that is required is that

$\dot{P}_d$ rise at a rate that does not exceed $\dot{P}_f + m$. The difference m can, of course, be zero or negative. It has been a fundamental tenet of American policy in recent years that m should be negative. The rise in the American price level must be kept below that of the European price level in order to improve our competitive position and thus eventually restore balance-of-payments equilibrium.

Most of the countries in Western Europe have been able to permit their domestic price levels to rise moderately rapidly, since for each of them $\dot{P}_f$ was also rising, and thus m could be kept close to zero. The German revaluation in 1961 represents an exception. The German balance-of-payments surplus might have been eliminated by taking m as a significant positive figure— that is, by encouraging the domestic price level to rise faster than that in other countries. Instead, the mark was revalued upward.

3. Now we come to the third way in which the behavior of the price level influences policy. There is some upper limit to the rise in the price level beyond which the functioning of the economy is impaired—through speculation, the development of politically disturbing inequities in the distribution of wealth and income, and the beginnings of a "flight from the currency." This is the rationale usually offered, over and above that involving the balance of payments, for seeking to maintain a stable price level. Germany is the country in which presumably this rationale operates most strongly to influence policy.

We expressed this constraint in the form

$$\dot{P} \leqslant n$$

The odds are that n has a higher value than is generally assumed, and no country in Western Europe has come close to it in the last decade. It would appear that n has had a lower value in the United States in the postwar period than in most European countries.[28]

The situation may be stated in another way. Whatever the value of n, it is a powerful constraint if and when it is brought into operation. The governments of the advanced economies on both sides of the Atlantic would feel obliged to make substantial sacrifices in terms of both employment and growth if they thought that inflation threatened to get out of control (apart from balance-of-payments difficulties) and that deflationary policies were necessary to prevent the rise in prices from exceeding their estimate of n. However, on the whole, this has not happened in the postwar period.

Thus, during the last decade or more, price stability as an aggregative goal has operated primarily as what we have called a "second-order constraint," as a constraint imposed by the need to satisfy the primary balance-of-payments constraint. As a result, the goal has, in fact, taken the form, not of absolute stability of the domestic price level, but of approximate constancy in the relation between domestic and foreign price levels. Stability in the domestic price level itslf has entered positively—but, on the whole, not very strongly—into policy makers' welfare functions. This accounts for the official statements frequently heard that the domestic price level should not rise more than, say, 2 per cent per year; but it is fair to say that no Western European government—not even Germany—would be prepared to sacrifice much employment to bring the rise in prices down from 4 or 3 per cent per annum to 2 per cent if not forced to do so by the balance-of-payments constraint.[29]

Incomes Policy

Let us now turn to "incomes policy," which can be covered here only very briefly. "Incomes policy" is a polite way of referring to a policy of wage restraint with a *quid pro quo*—the latter taking the form of some restraint on other incomes, particularly profits.[30] In terms of our welfare formulation, we might perhaps say that we have here to some extent a negative constraint of the third order; that is, wage restraint helps to meet the price constraint which is a condition for satisfaction of the balance-of-payments constraint. As the OECD has put it, "The purpose of incomes policies is . . . to control the development of costs and prices."[31]

Wage restraint may serve other purposes in addition to protecting the balance of payments through its contribution to

greater price stability. In France, for example, the rapid rise
in wages has apparently reduced profit margins and the amount
of business profits available for reinvestment. Reinvested profits
play a crucial role in French planning for rapid economic growth.
In this case a successful incomes policy, if it not only restrained
wage increases but also brought about some shift from wages
to profits, would contribute to growth as well as to price stability
and balance-of-payments equilibrium.[32] Obviously, such a policy
is hardly likely to command the support of a strong and independent labor movement.[33]

Emphasis on incomes policy is a relatively new development
in Europe.[34] It has been paralleled in the United States by the
formulation of the "wage-price guideposts" in the January 1962
Economic Report of the President. The new emphasis on wage
restraint reflects the growing inflationary pressures in most European countries and the search for methods of price restraint—
from the side of costs—that would not entail the threat to the
employment and growth goals that would arise from relying
only on restriction of aggregate demand through monetary and
fiscal policy.[35]

It is clear from the continued upward pressure on prices in
most European countries that incomes policy has thus far not
provided a very effective constraint. No country has succeeded
in keeping wages from rising faster than productivity. Indeed,
whatever the official statements, no government has, in fact,
tried to enforce such a stringent requirement over a succession
of years. We must remember that an incomes policy is merely
a means to a means to an end. If rising prices abroad permit
prices at home to rise without balance-of-payments difficulties,
then there is no need to keep wage increases strictly in line
with productivity increases. It will be remembered that we formulated our expression for the incomes goal as

$$\dot{W} - \dot{y} \leqslant \dot{P}_f + m \pm g$$

If foreign prices are rising, wages can rise faster than productivity, subject to whatever differential (m) between the trends in
domestic and foreign prices the government wants to maintain.
It has been the hope of the American government that this country could maintain a negative m, virtually as large as the rate

of increase in foreign prices, so as to improve our competitive position. This does imply holding wage increases down to the rise in average labor productivity. During the last few years, increasing balance-of-payments difficulties have forced some European countries to try to reduce the value of m to zero or lower—and it is in this recent period that the emphasis on incomes policy has developed.[36] The most dramatic recent example of the development of an incomes policy was that of the British Labor Government in the second half of 1966. An earlier attempt, involving the establishment of a National Incomes Commission in Britain, in 1962, had failed to slow down the rise in wages and prices.[37]

Some countries, notably The Netherlands, have consciously had and tried to enforce an incomes policy during some part of the postwar period.[38] The term is not officially used in the United States; but, as we have already noted, the "wage-price guideposts," formulated in the January 1962 *Economic Report of the President*, amount in effect to the statement of an incomes policy. These guidelines have been repeated in subsequent *Economic Reports*. During 1962–1964, with the help of an unemployment rate above 5 per cent, the guideposts made some contribution to the relative stability of wages and prices. But as unemployment fell toward and then below 4 per cent in 1965–1966, the rise in wages and prices accelerated, and resistance to the guideposts by both labor and business grew stronger.

In one important respect, incomes policy stands on a different footing from our other aggregative policies. In economies which emphasize free collective bargaining, the means may not exist for effectively implementing the policy. In the absence of centralized wage bargaining on a national scale, with some direct influence by government, an incomes policy is merely—as it has been characterized by the Council of Economic Advisers—a set of guideposts. But, as an OECD report has put it, "Once the guidance has been given, the problem is to get people to follow it, and to do so without damage to democratic values. Many governments have moved very cautiously on incomes policy because of their awareness of the difficulty of securing the necessary cooperation, and of the embarrassing situation which arises if they offer specific guidance which is then rejected."[39] This is true on both sides of the Atlantic.[40]

Rapid Growth as a Goal

We now come to what we may call our two positive aggregative goals—full employment and rapid economic growth. The first we shall reserve for extended discussion in the next two chapters. Here, we shall deal briefly with the goal of rapid economic growth.[41] It is not surprising that economic growth should be stressed more in Europe than in the United States. Here again a ratchet effect has been at work. Initial success in generating rapid, sustained growth has led to firm resolves not to permit relapses into relative stagnation—although it is recognized that some of the spectacular growth rates of the past decade cannot be maintained indefinitely.[42]

The new emphasis on growth in the United Kingdom, reflected in the establishment of the National Economic Development Council in early 1962 represents an interesting example of a conscious reformulation of the way national welfare is related to our aggregative target variables. A new emphasis was put on growth, and an incomes policy was officially formulated for the first time.[43] (As we have already seen, this effort to establish an incomes policy was not successful.) Parallel with these restatements of policy objectives went an interesting reexamination of the probable relationships among the target variables. The balance-of-payments constraint remained unchallenged, and the price constraint continued as a means of ensuring external balance. However, there has been a new emphasis on achieving relative price stability by accelerating the increase in productivity through stimulating economic growth.[44] This, in turn, has implied the need for an incomes policy to hold wage increases in line with the rise in productivity. Otherwise the balance-of-payments constraint would from time to time require restrictive measures that would retard or halt growth and increase unemployment. This indeed happened in 1965–1966 as on previous occasions in British postwar experience. In 1966 the British government was forced to adopt strong deflationary measures, which temporarily increased unemployment and retarded growth, while at the same time it moved much more vigorously than in 1962 to impose an incomes policy. Further steps were also taken to accelerate the rate of increase in labor productivity, and thus the rate of growth in potential output.

In the last few years, the United States has come to place more emphasis on the goal of rapid economic growth than was placed before, say, 1962.[45] It is fair to say, however, that the way the growth goal is viewed is still somewhat different on the two sides of the Atlantic. In Europe, the government's ability and willingness to ensure that aggregate demand expands as rapidly as potential output are taken for granted. The emphasis is placed, instead, on what may be considered as the *supply* aspects of the problem of stimulating growth. That is, efforts are directed toward accelerating the growth of productive capacity, for example, through measures that increase the ratio of investment to GNP and that improve the skills and mobility of the work force. In the United States, on the other hand, the new accent on growth emphasizes the need to ensure that aggregate demand rises as rapidly as potential output and that unemployment is kept down to the level defined by the goal of full employment. The rise in potential output has largely been taken as given, although in the last few years there has been a heavier emphasis than before on stimulating the growth of potential output through incentives to private investment and through manpower measures that would, among other effects, accelerate the rise in average labor productivity.

NOTES

1. We can only note in passing that all of these economic objectives are related to, and instrumental in the furthering of, political and philosophic goals—personal freedom, political order and stability, national prestige, etc. With respect to the goals of economic policy, see E. S. Kirschen et al., *Economic Policy in Our Time* (Chicago: Rand McNally, 1964), Vol. I, Chaps. 1, 9; and E. S. Kirschen and L. Morissens, "The Objectives and Instruments of Economic Policy," in B. G. Hickman (ed.), *Quantitative Planning of Economic Policy* (Washington: The Brookings Institution, 1965), pp. 111–133.

2. Fiscal and monetary policy are to be interpreted broadly as including also national debt policy.

3. We shall refer to the nature of this relationship at various points in the present volume and at some length in Chapter 7. A review of

some of the evidence bearing on the relations among the target variables corresponding to our aggregative economic goals is provided by L. R. Klein and R. G. Bodkin in their paper in Commission on Money and Credit, *Inflation, Growth, and Employment* (Englewood Cliffs, New Jersey: Prentice-Hall, 1964). Some of the other papers in this book are also useful in this connection. See also Note 23.

4. Thus, ". . . it is becoming increasingly clear that a strong domestic economy is a condition for a solution of the balance of payments problem and that there is much less conflict between internal and external policy requirements than might be thought. Organization for Economic Co-operation and Development, *Economic Surveys by the OECD: United States* (Paris: OECD, 1963), p. 15.

5. See, for example, Kirschen et al., *op. cit.,* pp. 226–229, and Kirschen and Morissens, *op. cit.,* p. 130.

6. Jack Downie, "The Importance of Knowing What You Want," in A. M. Ross (ed.), *Unemployment and the American Economy* (New York: John Wiley and Sons, 1964), p. 162.

7. The phrase "target variable" is borrowed from Jan Tinbergen. See his book, *On the Theory of Economic Policy* (Amsterdam: North-Holland Publishing Company, 1952), pp. 1, 6.

8. As we shall argue later, employment policy should aim not at merely one unemployment rate for the entire labor force but at an entire set or matrix of unemployment rates for different segments of the labor force. However, for our present purpose, it is sufficient to confine our attention to the single aggregative target variable, the national unemployment rate.

9. It might also be expressed in terms of a desired rate of increase in real GNP per capita.

10. "It is difficult, on purely logical grounds, to conceive of a policy which does not have as an aim the maximization of a social welfare function—subject, of course, to constraints imposed by political or other considerations." *Economic Planning in Europe* (Geneva: United Nations, 1965), Chap. 2, p. 1. This book was also published as Part 2 of *Economic Survey of Europe, 1962.*

11. As we shall see later, the targets are sometimes so inflexible that we can properly speak of constraints rather than variables. Usually, when quantitative targets are set, they are not absolutely inflexible, and the statement of the target can be interpreted as a crude approximation of some of the characteristics of the welfare function. Thus, setting a target for the unemployment rate suggests that little or no increase in welfare occurs as the unemployment rate falls below this target, particularly if effects on other variables relevant to welfare are taken into account.

12. The notion of a social (or economic) welfare function developed here is only a distant cousin of the social welfare function that has played such a prominent role in the recent literature dealing with the pure theory of economic welfare. The notion of a social welfare function considered by, for example, Bergson and Arrow represents an attempt

to relate the social desirability of different "social states" to the orders of preference for these states implied by the different tastes of all the individuals in society. The question asked is: Is it "formally possible to construct a procedure for passing from a set of known individual tastes to a pattern of social decision-making, the procedure in question being required to satisfy certain natural conditions"?

The discussion is entirely in classical, microeconomic terms. That is, the "social states" considered consist of the outputs and prices of individual commodities produced by different firms, the prices and inputs of individual productive factors employed by different firms, and the incomes and amounts of each commodity bought by all individuals. The problem posed is to derive a set of social rankings out of the possible ways in which these microvariables can be combined, given the tastes of all individuals in society, and to do so without making interpersonal comparisons of utility that imply value judgments. For a useful review of this literature, see E. J. Mishan, "A Survey of Welfare Economics, 1939–1959," *Economic Journal*, LXX (June 1960), 197–265. The quotation is from Kenneth J. Arrow, *Social Choice and Individual Values* (New York: John Wiley and Sons, 1951), p. 2.

In contrast to this treatment, our approach to a social welfare function disregards the link between social welfare and individual tastes and reflects only the ordering of the preferences of the policy maker (or observer) for the different possible combinations of variables ("social states") that are considered. Furthermore, we deal only with aggregates and thereby exclude consideration of allocation and distribution problems. For a somewhat similar approach, see J. Tinbergen, *Economic Policy: Principles and Design* (Amsterdam: North-Holland Publishing Company, 1956), Chap. 1; also Hickman (ed.), *op. cit.*, especially the essay by Theil; and H. Theil, *Economic Forecasts and Policy* (Amsterdam: North-Holland Publishing Company, 1961).

13. Tibor Scitovsky, "On the Principle of Consumers' Sovereignty," *American Economic Review*, LII (May 1962), 268.

14. A comment by Paul Samuelson seems relevant here: "The social welfare function is a concept as broad and empty as language itself—and as necessary." In B. F. Haley (ed.), *A Survey of Contemporary Economics*, Vol. II (Homewood, Ill.: Irwin, 1952), p. 37.

15. We have expressed the policy maker's welfare function only in terms of the target variables, such as unemployment and the rate of change in output and in the price level. This is incomplete, since the policy maker's "instrument variables"—such as tax rates, the amount of government expenditures, and so on—also enter into the welfare function and must be considered in arriving at an optimal solution. For our purposes, however, since we are not concerned with formal solutions, the incomplete formulation in the text is sufficient. In the next chapter, we shall briefly consider how one or more fiscal instrumental variables presumably have entered into the welfare function of American policy makers. For a more formal and complete statement that brings both target and instrument

variables into the welfare function, see H. Theil, "Linear Decision Rules for Macrodynamic Policy Problems," in Hickman (ed.), *op. cit.*, pp. 18–42.

16. In this connection, see Note 15. Welfare is affected not only by changes in the target variables but also by changes in the instrument variables (such as government spending) which are used to change the target variables.

17. For a similar distinction between full employment as a "final objective" and price stability and balance-of-payments equilibrium as "means-to-end-objectives," see C. Weststrate, *Economic Policy in Practice: The Netherlands 1950/1957* (Leiden: H. E. Stenfert Kroese, 1959), especially pp. 7–8. Tinbergen also treats the balance-of-payments deficit as, in effect, a constraint. In his terms, it is a target that takes the form of a condition—the condition, for example, that the deficit be equal to zero. See, *On the Theory of Economic Policy*, p. 9. See also *Economic Planning in Europe*, Chap. 2, p. 1.

18. See Walter S. Salant et al., *The United States Balance of Payments in 1968* (Washington: The Brookings Institution, 1963) for a good discussion of the role of the balance-of-payments constraint on both sides of the Atlantic. Other useful sources are the annual economic surveys of member countries by the Organization for Economic Co-operation and Development and the annual volumes of *Economic Survey of Europe* published by the United Nations. See also Kirschen et al., *op. cit.*

19. There is, of course, a voluminous literature on the balance-of-payments difficulties of the United States in recent years. See in particular the volume by Salant and others already cited and Hal B. Lary, *Problems of the United States as World Trader and Banker* (New York: National Bureau of Economic Research, 1963). For a critical review of these two volumes as well as references to some of the other relevant literature, see Harry G. Johnson, "The International Competitive Position of the United States and the Balance of Payments Prospect for 1968," *Review of Economics and Statistics,* **XLVI** (February 1964), 14–32. See also *Balance of Payments—1965,* Hearings before a Subcommittee of the Senate Committee on Banking nad Currency, 89th Congress, 1st session (1965).

20. For a defense of official policy, see the testimony of Robert B. Roosa in *Outlook for United States Balance of Payments,* Hearings before the Subcommittee on International Exchange and Payments of the Joint Economic Committee, 87th Congress, 2nd session (1963), pp. 117–118. See also W. McC. Martin, "Monetary Policy and International Payments," *Journal of Finance,* **XVIII** (March 1963), 1–10. For one of the more vigorous recent attacks on government policy, particularly in the monetary field, see J. M. Culbertson, *Full Employment or Stagnation?* (New York: McGraw-Hill, 1964).

21. See, for example, the alternative proposals in Walter S. Salant et al., *op. cit.,* Chap. IX. See also the *Hearings* cited in Note 20 as well as the compilation of studies prepared for the same Subcommittee under the title, *Factors Affecting the United States Balance of Payments,* 87th Congress, 2nd session (1962).

22. See the statement in Note 4, which is taken from *Economic Surveys by the OECD: United States*, p. 15. See also Salant et al., *op. cit.*, p. 126.

23. This, for example, is the position taken in William Fellner et al., *The Problem of Rising Prices* (Paris: OECD, 1961). It might be argued that the prevailing view in most countries, particularly among those groups with some influence on policy, is that the optimum rate of change in the price level is not zero but some positive number—say, 1 or 2 per cent per year—because the moderate stimulus thus provided to economic activity more than offsets, in its effects on welfare, the redistributional effects which benefit debtors at the expense of creditors and those on fixed incomes. Contrast this view with the unqualified declaration that "rising prices are not compatible with steady growth" in Fellner et al., *op. cit.*, p. 75.

Among economists, Neil Jacoby may be correct that the prevailing view seems to be that "creeping inflation . . . is in the long run a drag upon national progress, and that it is both feasible and desirable to prevent its occurrence." See S. S. Alexander et al., *Economics and the Policy Maker* (Washington: The Brookings Institution, 1959), p. 48; also the references on p. 49. However, a number of economists have expressed the opposite view. For a useful survey of the evidence which suggests that a mild upward trend in prices stimulates growth, see the paper by R. G. Bodkin in S. F. Kaliski (ed.), *Canadian Economic Policy Since the War* (Ottawa: Canadian Trade Committee, 1960), especially pp. 50–54.

24. "Clearly, no Member country would be willing to accept high levels of unemployment in order to hold its prices in check." *Policies for Price Stability* (Paris: OECD, 1962), p. 15. Germany seems to be a partial exception. The official emphasis on price stability in that country is well known, and it is probably true, as Herr Erhard declared in his 1963 Economic Report to the Bundestag, that some economic growth would be sacrificed in the interest of greater price stability, apart from balance-of-payments considerations. However, it is not clear that any significant amount of employment would be sacrificed. My own observations lead me to doubt that it would be considered politically possible to permit the unemployment rate to rise much above, say, 2 per cent in order to slow down the rise in prices. This was admitted to me by more than one German official. In this connection, it is interesting to note the criticism by the newly appointed Board of Experts in its report for 1964 that the conflict between full employment and price stability in Germany had been resolved in favor of full employment. See the summary of the Board's report in *The German Economic Review*, **III** (1965), especially p. 75.

25. Germany and the United States are sometimes linked together in the relative importance they place on price stability, apart from balance-of-payments considerations.

26. There is another respect in which the goal of price stability affects policy action in the United States. American policy has had to be con-

cerned with the problem of cyclical instability in general economic activity
in the postwar period, to a greater extent than European policy. Prevention
of rapid price increases on cyclical upswings becomes a means of minimizing speculative excesses and other maladjustments and thus of minimizing
the duration and amplitude of subsequent cyclical contractions. These
considerations have obviously been important in Federal Reserve thinking.

27. The following statement from OECD is worth quoting in this connection. The greater emphasis on the need for price stability in Europe
since the beginning of the 1960's exists because "rising prices are seen
to be a threat to the achievement of other objectives of policy, such
as full employment, economic growth, or a satisfactory distribution of
income. In particular, . . . the pursuit of successful employment and
growth policies in any particular country has become more dependent
on its success in keeping its economic conditions broadly in line with
those prevailing elsewhere, and especially keeping its price level in line."
Policies for Price Stability, p. 19. For a similar emphasis in the Canadian
situation, see David C. Smith, "The Canadian Full Employment Goal,"
The Canadian Banker, **LXXI** (Winter, 1964), 11–12.

28. It was previously suggested (Note 26) that the monetary authorities
in the United States seem to place a good deal of importance on the
need to restrict the rise in prices during cyclical expansions, apart from
balance-of-payments considerations. This concern with the interrelations
between rising prices and cyclical instability is likely to lead, at least
in the short run, to placing a lower value on n than would be placed
if the concern of the monetary authorities were more vaguely conceived
in terms of a flight from the currency and severe inequities in the distribution of the burden of inflation.

29. A qualification is needed here. If overfull employment existed, a
government would be prepared to permit a modest rise in unemployment
in order to restrain the rise in prices. The labor market could be so
tight that a slight rise in unemployment would be considered as adding
to, rather than subtracting from, total welfare. This has, in fact, been
the case recently in Germany and some other European countries.

30. The problems involved in seeking to control nonwage incomes are
reviewed in the OECD report on *Policies for Prices, Profits, and Other
Non-Wage Incomes* (Paris: OECD, 1964). For a recent useful survey
of incomes policies, with an excellent bibliography, see David C. Smith,
*Incomes Policies: Some Foreign Experiences and Their Relevance for
Canada* (Ottawa: Queen's Printer, 1966).

31. *Policies for Economic Growth* (Paris: OECD, 1962), p. 38. Some
readers may prefer not to think of incomes policy as reflecting a macroeconomic goal in the same sense as the other goals considered in this
chapter, but rather, like fiscal policy, as merely the use of particular
instrument variables (in this case wages and pofits) to bring about desired
values of target variables such as the rate of change in prices.

32. See Bela Balassa, "Whither French Planning?" *Quarterly Journal
of Economics*, **LXXIX** (November 1965), 537–554. While the need for

some variant of an incomes policy has been emphasized in France, the French have been no more successful than other countries in formulating and maintaining a successful incomes policy. Among the various official sources on this subject, in addition to the parliamentary debates on the Fourth and Fifth Plans, see the "Massé Report," *Rapport sur la Politique des Revenues Établi à la suite de la Conférence des Revenus* (Paris: La Documentation Française, 1964). Recuelis et Monographies No. 47. See also David C. Smith, *op. cit.,* Chap. 8.

33. It should be noted that French concern with incomes policy involves not only promoting price stability and reinvestment of profits to accelerate growth but also some redistribution of income in favor of less privileged groups.

34. See *World Economic Survey, 1964* (New York: United Nations, 1965), part II, pp. 41 ff., and *Economic Survey of Europe in 1963,* Part 1, Chap. 2, pp. 71–75. The need for a national wages policy was strongly recommended to OECD countries in Fellner et al., *op. cit.,* particularly pp. 55 ff. See also the OECD report which followed: *Policies for Price Stability,* especially pp. 23–47. The Netherlands is one country which consciously had and implemented a national wages policy from the end of World War II.

35. While it is correct to say that there has been a new emphasis on the need for an incomes policy in recent years, recognition of the need for wage restraint under conditions of full employment and concern about the "cost-push" aspect of inflation go back to the early postwar years. It is still interesting, in this connection, to reread the Swedish debate in Ralph Turvey (ed.), *Wages Policy Under Full Employment* (London: William Hodge, 1952).

36. See, for example, *Policies for Price Stability,* especially pp. 23 ff.

37. Efforts to obtain the cooperation of labor and industry in 1964–1965 in restraining wage and price increases were largely unsuccessful. For a survey of British postwar attempts to restrain the rise in wages and prices, see Murray Edelman and R. W. Fleming, *The Politics of Wage-Price Decisions* (Urbana, Ill.: University of Illinois Press, 1965), Chap. 4; also David C. Smith, *op. cit.,* Chap. 5. The 1966 experience can be followed in *The Economist.* See also Lloyd Ulman, "Under Severe Restraint: British Incomes Policy," *Industrial Relations, VI* (May, 1967), 213–266. For an excellent general review of postwar British stabilization policy to 1960, see J. C. R. Dow, *The Management of the British Economy, 1945–60* (Cambridge: Cambridge University Press, 1964).

38. The Dutch policy of wage restraint, which had some success during most of the postwar period, has recently run into serious difficulties. See *The Economist,* March 28, 1964, pp. 1273–1274 and April 16, 1966, pp. 281–282, and the recent annual *Economic Surveys* of The Netherlands by the OECD. For a history of Dutch incomes policy since the war, see Fellner et al., *op. cit.,* pp. 359–390; Edelman and Fleming, *op. cit.,* Chap. 5, and David C. Smith, *op. cit.,* Chap. 6.

39. *Policies for Price Stability,* p. 35. See also Edelman and Fleming,

op cit. In October 1966, the British government stopped relying on voluntary cooperation and, by putting into effect Part 4 of the Prices and Incomes Act, imposed a temporary but compulsory freeze on wages and prices.

40. In Sweden in 1963, "the authorities contemplate neither direct intervention in wage negotiations nor the issue of recommendations as to the sort of wage increases compatible with price stability. This attitude is based partly on general political principles. But it is also felt that any official guidance as to the general scope for wage increases would tend to be regarded not as averages, but as minima to which special claims from individual groups would be added." *Economic Surveys by the OECD: Sweden* (Paris: OECD, 1963), pp. 17–18.

41. See Angus Maddison, *Economic Growth in the West* (New York: Twentieth Century Fund, 1964), and *Policies for Economic Growth.* For a useful brief survey of long-term plans in Western Europe, which by now is not completely up to date, see *Economic Bulletin for Europe,* **XIV** (November 1962), published by the United Nations. For a more detailed review, see *Economic Planning in Europe.* See also the survey of economic planning in a number of European countries in *Weltwirtschaftliches Archiv,* Band 92, Heft 1 (1964).

42. For a useful survey of postwar growth trends and policies, see Maddison, *op. cit.; Economic Survey of Europe in 1961, Part 2, Some Factors in Economic Growth in Europe During the 1950's* (Geneva: United Nations, 1964); and OECD, *Economic Growth, 1960–1970* (Paris: OECD, 1966).

43. See National Economic Development Council, *Growth of the United Kingdom Economy to 1966* (London: HMSO, 1963) and *Conditions Favourable to Faster Growth* (London: HMSO, 1963); also *Incomes Policy: The Next Step,* Cmd. 1626 (London: HMSO, 1962), and Dow, *op. cit.,* Chap. 16. See also *Economic Surveys by the OECD: United Kingdom* (Paris: OECD, 1963). This change in emphasis is said to have begun with proposals put forward in Parliament by Selwyn Lloyd in 1961. See *British Parliamentary Debates (Hansard): House of Commons,* 5th Series, Vol. 645, July 24–August 4, 1961 (London: HMSO, 1961), pp. 218 ff. Another interesting example of a shift in the priorities attached to the various aggregative goals is to be found in Belgium. Increased emphasis was put on the employment goal from the mid-fifties on, and in the late fifties a new importance came to be attached to the growth objective. A similar new emphasis on the goal of rapid growth has occurred in The Netherlands.

44. See *Conditions Favourable to Faster Growth,* p. 47.

45. This seems to be also true of Canada. See Economic Council of Canada, *First Annual Review: Economic Goals for Canada* (Ottawa: Queen's Printer, 1964).

CHAPTER 3

Full Employment
as a Policy Goal

Price stability and balance-of-payments equilibrium have long been recognized as appropriate economic goals for national governments to follow. Full employment, however, is a relatively recent addition to the list of aggregative economic goals. Indeed, before the Great Depression no government in the world officially accepted responsibility for maintaining a high and stable level of employment.[1]

Before the Great Depression

In the United States, before the 1930's, the maintenance of a high level of employment was not considered to be a primary responsibility of the federal government, and the situation was not much different in other industrial countries. The term "full employment" had not yet come into circulation among economists, much less among men in the street or in political life. The human problems resulting from unemployment "were left to local and usually private charities; the course of the trade cycle was left to God and economic 'laws.' "[2]

It is true that in 1921 a President's Conference on Unemployment was held under the chairmanship of Herbert Hoover, then Secretary of Commerce, thereby setting something of a precedent for the future; but little in the way of either federal action

or federal acceptance of responsibility emerged from the conference. Indeed, the attitude of the federal government at the time
was presumably expressed by President Harding in his welcom-
ing speech at the conference: "There has been vast unemployment before and there will be again. There will be depression
and inflation just as surely as the tides ebb and flow. I would
have little enthusiasm for any proposed remedy which seeks
either palliation or tonic from the Public Treasury."[3] This view
was supplemented by Secretary Hoover in the following words:[4]

> The Administration has felt that a large degree of solu-
> tion could be expected through the mobilization of the fine
> cooperative action of our manufacturers and employers, of
> our public bodies and local authorities, and that if a solution
> could be found in these directions we should have accom-
> plished even more than the care of our unemployed, that we
> will have again demonstrated that independence and ability
> of action amongst our own people that saves our Govern-
> ment from that ultimate paternalism that will undermine
> our whole political life.

In 1909, William Beveridge, the noted British economist, published a book, which has become something of a classic, entitled
Unemployment: A Problem of Industry.[5] While the book was
concerned with British conditions, the title expresses also the
prevailing American attitude at the beginning of the 1920's. That
attitude can be summarized as follows: Unemployment, beyond
what could be removed by better organization of the labor market, was a product of the business cycle. Business fluctuations
could be ameliorated by improved business planning with the
help of better statistical information. Evening out private and
local public construction would help, as would a national system
of employment exchanges to improve the mobility of workers.
A fundamental assumption was that the role of the central government should be kept to a minimum.[6]
  Beveridge's book applied to conditions in England before the
Great Depression. As in the *Report of the Royal Commission
on the Poor Laws and the Relief of Distress* (1909), emphasis
was placed on the need for improving the organization of the

labor market through a national system of employment exchanges. The need for a national system of unemployment insurance was also stressed. Both of these steps had been taken by
the British government before the outbreak of World War I.
The Royal Commission (and Beveridge) also pointed out the
possibilities of stabilizing employment by advance planning and
regularization of expenditures on public works. But nowhere in
Beveridge's classic, even in its 1930 edition, is there any statement of the employment objective in the form it was to acquire
in his later famous report on *Full Employment in a Free Society*,
namely, that "the ultimate responsibility for seeing that outlay
as a whole, taking public and private outlay together, is sufficient
to set up a demand for all the labor seeking employment, must
be taken by the State . . ."[7] In other words, it is the responsibility of the central government to maintain aggregate demand
at a level to ensure full employment. But this was not the general
view in England, on the Continent, or in the United States when
the Great Depression struck.

From the Great Depression to the Employment Act

Between 1929 and 1931 unemployment in the United States
rose spectacularly—from between 3 and 4 per cent of the labor
force to about 16 per cent. A year later the figure was 24 per
cent. At the bottom of the depression in 1933 a full quarter
of the American labor force was without jobs.[8] And until 1933,
the position of Congress and the Administration continued to
be essentially as it had been in the 1920's: It was not the responsibility of the federal government either to relieve the distress
resulting from unemployment or to take direct action aimed
at reducing unemployment. Neither the hesitant attempt "to
provide for the advance planning and regulated construction
of public works" in the Employment Stabilization Act of 1931
nor the provision of funds to states and local governments
through the Emergency Relief and Construction Act of 1932
is more than a minor exception to this generalization.[9]

All this changed radically, of course, with the coming of the
New Deal. We need not review in detail the variety of measures

and agencies with which the federal government sought, first, to cope with the distress resulting from mass unemployment and, second, to stimulate the economy toward higher levels of employment. Such abbreviations as CCC, FERA, PWA, CWA, and WPA are probably still familiar to those who lived through those hectic years—not to mention the ill-fated NRA.[10] After an initial and brief commitment to a balanced budget, the Roosevelt Administration entered into a vigorous program of deficit spending—for both relief and public works—at the same time that other measures were taken to stimulate recovery, ranging from devaluation of the dollar and efforts to raise wages and prices to large-scale financial support in such areas as agriculture and home-financing. Yet, from the point of view of achieving full employment, the inadequacy of these measures is reflected in the fact that at the end of the 1930's the national unemployment rate was still in the neighborhood of 15 per cent.

The Great Depression forced the United States and other governments into accepting responsibility for supporting and raising the level of employment. The theoretical rationale for the government's assuming such responsibility was provided by J. M. Keynes' *The General Theory of Employment, Interest, and Money*. Employment depends on the level of aggregate demand (that is, total spending on goods and services), but the economy does not inevitably tend toward an equilibrium level of demand high enough to generate jobs for all those who want to work. Total spending may need to be stimulated through government action—particularly through fiscal policy. Tax changes can directly affect private spending (consumption and private investment), and government expenditures can add directly to aggregate demand, as well as contribute to private spending indirectly through multiplier effects. Keynes' classic let loose a flood of literature on how to maintain a full employment level of aggregate demand which has not yet subsided.[11] Later, during World War II, the same tools of analysis were used to cope with the problem of inflation; and still later, during the 1950's and 1960's, these tools were turned to studying how to maintain full employment within a context of rapid economic growth, while at the same time avoiding any significant degree of inflation.

The decade of the thirties ended with Hitler's march into

TABLE 3.1. Unemployment Rates in Various Countries, 1928-1938 (per cent)

Year	Belgium	Germany	Italy	Netherlands	Sweden	United Kingdom	United States
1928	0.6	3.8	---	1.6	2.4	6.1	4.2
1929	0.8	5.9	1.7	1.7	2.4	5.9	3.2
1930	2.2	9.5	2.5	2.3	3.3	9.3	8.9
1931	6.8	13.9	4.3	4.3	4.8	12.6	16.3
1932	11.9	17.2	5.8	8.3	6.8	13.1	24.1
1933	10.6	14.8	5.9	9.7	7.3	11.7	25.2
1934	11.8	8.3	5.6	9.8	6.4	9.9	22.0
1935	11.1	6.5	---	11.2	6.2	9.2	20.3
1936	8.4	4.8	---	11.9	5.3	7.9	17.0
1937	7.2	2.7	5.0	10.5	5.1	6.7	14.3
1938	8.7	1.3	4.6	9.9	5.1	8.1	19.1

Sources: For the United States, from Stanley Lebergott, Manpower in Economic Growth (New York: McGraw-Hill, 1964), p. 512; all others from Angus Maddison, Economic Growth in the West (New York: Twentieth Century Fund, 1964), p. 220.

Poland, and all-out war quickly created the jobs which peacetime economies had not been able to generate. Table 3.1 presents some figures on unemployment in a number of countries in the decade preceding the outbreak of World War II.

With the exception of Germany, which was already substantially on a war footing, none of the countries listed had been able by 1937-1938 to bring unemployment down to the levels prevailing at the end of the 1920's. The 1938 figures in Table 3.1 are affected in varying degrees by the recession of 1937-1938, which affected the United States—and to a lesser extent Belgium and the United Kingdom—more than the other countries listed.

Spurred by the continuing high level of unemployment and by the intellectual stimulus of the "Keynesian Revolution," an increasing number of economists and research groups in the late 1930's—particularly in England, Sweden, and the United States—turned their attention to ways of achieving and maintaining full employment. Then came the war, and with it the actual achievement of full employment. The war brought also concern about the problem of postwar readjustment and a widespread resolve, both in and out of government, that in the years ahead a paramount goal of public policy should be the maintenance of a high level of employment—of full employment. This resolve had spread so widely among nations by the end of the war that the goal of full employment was written into the United Nations Charter (Article 55).[12]

In the United States, the National Planning Association (a private group), the Fiscal Division of the Bureau of the Budget, and the National Resources Planning Board were among the earliest groups to emphasize governmental responsibility for maintaining a high and stable level of employment.[13] The question of maintaining employment after the war was debated in Congressional hearings concerned with setting up machinery for reconversion to a peacetime economy when the war ended. In the presidential campaign of 1944, both political parties made gestures toward the goal of high and stable employment. The Democratic platform boldly pledged the party to "guarantee full employment." The Republicans, more cautiously, promised to "promote the fullest stable employment through private enterprise." Actually, the Republican candidate went much further. "We must have full employment," he said. And, in another speech, he added: "That is everybody's business. Therefore it is the business of government."[14]

In January 1945, Senator Murray introduced his Full Employment Bill. Thirteen months later, after much Congressional soul-searching, many amendments, and much rewriting, the Employment Act of 1946 became law. The phrase "full employment" is nowhere mentioned in the act as passed, which declared that:

> . . . it is the continuing policy and responsibility of the Federal Government to use all practical means consistent with its needs and obligations and other essential considerations of national policy, with the assistance and cooperation of industry, agriculture, labor, and State and local governments, to coordinate and utilize all its plans, functions, and resources for the purpose of creating and maintaining, in a manner calculated to foster and promote free competitive enterprise and the general welfare, conditions under which there will be afforded useful employment opportunities, including self-employment, for those able, willing, and seeking to work, and to promote maximum employment, production, and purchasing power.[15]

Whether the government was to be responsible for "maximum" or "full" employment, the United States moved into the postwar world with the charge placed upon the federal government to ensure that the economy would provide "useful employment for those able, willing, and seeking to work."

The Employment Goal in Other Countries

The drive, during the 1930's and the war years, to establish high and stable employment as a primary goal of economic policy occurred not only in the United States (and Canada) but on the other side of the Atlantic as well—and, indeed, also on the other side of the world in Australia and New Zealand.[16] Most of Western Europe emerged from the war with either a legal or a political commitment to the goal of full employment.[17] And, as we have seen, this goal was also embodied in the United Nations Charter.

One of the first of these national commitments to the goal of high employment was that made by the British government in its *White Paper on Employment Policy,* issued in May 1944. In this document, the government accepted "as one of their primary aims and responsibilities the maintenance of a high and stable level of employment after the war."[18] Sir William Beveridge, although he felt that the White Paper did not go far enough, termed it "a milestone in economic and political history."[19] This action by the British government certainly influenced the governments of a number of other countries as they developed their plans to live in a world no longer at war.

A profound impression was also made by Beveridge's report, *Full Employment in a Free Society,* which appeared almost simultaneously with the *White Paper.* Beveridge argued with vigor that the government should commit itself unqualifiedly to the goal of full employment; he offered a definition of full employment that still arouses debate ("having always more vacant jobs than unemployed men"); and he emphasized the need not only to maintain aggregate demand but also to control the location of industry and to improve the mobility of workers.[20] And in one blunt sentence, he summarized a revolution in economic thought that was sweeping through the advanced countries of the Western world. "Full employment cannot be won and held without a great extension of the responsibilities and powers of the State exercised through organs of the central Government."[21]

This "great extension of the responsibilities and power of the State" has, in fact, occurred, even in nonsocialist economies. Countries have varied widely in the extent to which they have engaged in detailed national planning, but virtually all of the advanced economies have placed on their central governments the responsibility for managing the level of aggregate demand in order to achieve the aggregative economic goals listed at the beginning of Chapter 2. And although these goals are all interrelated, it is fair to say that the goal of full employment is viewed as the most important.[22]

Quantifying the Employment Goal

How far must unemployment fall before a country achieves the goal of full employment? At this point, it is desirable to introduce the distinction between "aggregative full employment," on the one hand, and "aggregative *and* structural full employment," on the other. Aggregative full employment corresponds to the lowest level to which it is considered feasible to reduce the overall unemployment rate, given both some minimum of frictional unemployment and also the underlying structural factors that make some sectors of the labor force more vulnerable to unemployment than others. More briefly, aggregative full employment is defined on the assumption of a given amount of frictional and structural unemployment.[23]

Wherever there is a heterogeneous labor force, some degree of "structural" unemployment will always exist at aggregative full employment. We must therefore go on to the second step in formulating a satisfactorily comprehensive statement of the full employment objective. This second step involves an answer to the following question: How far is a government prepared to go in reducing the amount of structural unemployment that exists at aggregative full employment? The answer to this question, when costs and benefits are weighed on the scales of the policy makers' value system, yields what we may call aggregative *and* structural full employment. In the United States, aggregative full employment today is widely assumed to imply an overall unemployment rate of about 4 per cent. However, many also believe that unemployment may, by means of an intensive manpower policy, be brought down further to 3 per cent—at a cost worth incurring in terms of the benefits to be achieved.

For the present, we shall confine ourselves to the goal of aggregative full employment. This is the goal that governments seek to achieve through the appropriate management of aggregate demand, primarily through the use of monetary and fiscal policy. Let us now see what numbers (for the overall unemployment rate) are associated with the goal of aggregative full employment in the United States and other leading industrial countries.

Today, in Western Europe, 2 per cent unemployment is the target most frequently mentioned.[24] When translated into American definitions, this may mean an unemployment rate ranging from somewhat below 2 per cent to perhaps 3 per cent as a maximum. Virtually all countries are loath to announce an official quantitative target.[25] (The United States, during the Kennedy and Johnson Administrations, has been a notable exception to this generalization.) However, various scraps of evidence permit us to infer the approximate goals which motivate policy. From such scraps of evidence, it would appear that the goals in some of the leading European countries today, *expressed in terms of American definitions*, are, very roughly, somewhat as in the following tabulation.[26]

France	2.0–3.0%
Germany	1.0–2.0
Sweden	1.2–1.7
United Kingdom	2.0–3.0

We must emphasize that these very rough approximations are expressed in terms of American definitions. This makes a significant difference in the case of France and the United Kingdom, whose official figures must be adjusted upward to correspond to American concepts.[27] Hence, to Frenchmen or Englishmen, our estimates of the unemployment goals for these countries may seem somewhat on the high side.

None of these targets would be officially admitted by any of the countries listed.[28] And it may be that, in some instances, the estimates presented here understate the range within which the unemployment goal is presumed to fall. Nevertheless, there is a fair amount of evidence that the welfare functions that have implicitly conditioned policy action in European capitals in recent years suggest employment targets approximately as we have listed them.

The Employment Goal in the United States

Let us turn now to the problem of formulating a full employment target for the United States.[29] There has been a great deal of debate since the Employment Act was passed in 1946 concerning what the quantitative target should be in order to achieve "high," "maximum," or "full" employment. Most of the numbers bandied about fall in the range of 3 to 5 per cent of the civilian labor force.

The early reports of the Council of Economic Advisers suggested a moderate range around 4 per cent. Thus the January 1947 report referred to a then current unemployment rate of about 3.9 per cent as "close to the minimum unavoidable in a free economy of great mobility such as ours."[30] A year later, a rate of 3.6 per cent was referred to as "probably the practical minimum."[31] Again, toward the end of the first Eisenhower Administration, full employment was said to have been "practically reached" when the current monthly rate was about 3.6 per cent.[32] On the whole, it is fair to say that, between 1946 and 1961, official policy at least tacitly accepted a target goal in the neighborhood of 4 per cent. But the target was not made explicit. One might say that a range rather than a single figure served as a target—the range being from an unemployment rate slightly below 4 per cent to an upper limit that at times was probably close to 5 per cent.[33]

All this can be restated in terms of our welfare function. The official view assumed that, under reasonably favorable conditions with respect to the behavior of the other relevant variables (particularly the price level), welfare would rise as the unemployment rate fell, until the latter approximated a level of 4 per cent. But when the other target (and instrument) variables were taken into account, the value judgments of successive administrations—as well as their views as to how the target variables were related to each other—varied enough so that "maximum welfare solutions" did not always yield the same unemployment rate as an immediate policy goal.[34]

The debate of the last few years on whether "structural" unemployment has been worsening has had an effect on the way the full employment goal is viewed in some circles both in and out of Washington. Those who have leaned strongly toward the structuralist side have suggested that, *in the short run,* the aggregative full employment target has to be set at an unemployment rate higher than 4 per cent. In the long run, through various types of manpower policy centered on education, training and retraining, and the like, the structural-frictional minimum can be reduced until the country can again have a short-run target of 4 per cent or less. Although this view carries some weight in the halls of Congress, it did not represent the official position of the Kennedy or Johnson Administration.[35]

The employment goal became much more explicit with the advent of the Kennedy Administration.[36] A temporary target of 4 per cent was accepted by the Council of Economic Advisers. "In the existing economic circumstances," this was considered to be a "reasonable and prudent full employment target for stabilization policy." However, this was to be only an interim goal: "If we move firmly to reduce the impact of structural unemployment, we will be able to move the unemployment target steadily from 4 per cent to successively lower rates."[37] This continued to be the position of the Council of Economic Advisers in the Johnson Administration.

An even more explicit formulation of the employment goal was proposed in the recent report by Senator Clark's Subcommittee on Employment and Manpower, which recommended

. . . that it be declared the public policy of the United States to maintain a level of unemployment no higher than 3 per cent of the labor force. The year 1968 should be set as the target for attainment of this goal.[38]

Here, as in the 1962 *Economic Report,* the full employment goal is viewed as being approached in two ways: (1) through eliminating unemployment associated with a deficiency of aggregate demand, given the hard core of "frictional" and "structural" unemployment that presumably exists today, and (2) operating through an aggressive and integrated manpower policy to reduce this frictional-structural minimum from its presumed present level of about 4 per cent to approximately 3 per cent.

Statements from the White House or a Senate Committee do not by themselves determine *de facto* policy or fully reflect the goals implicit in such policy. In this respect, it is fair to say that a change has occurred in the United States since the early months of 1964. At the time of the income tax reduction in February 1964, the state of employment policy in the United States could have been described as follows. The 4 per cent target was official policy. In Congress, as well as in the Administration, welfare was assumed to increase significantly as unemployment fell from, say, 6 per cent to below 5 per cent. But the slowness in getting the tax cut, the official and public concern with the balance of payments, continued worry in Congress and large sectors of public opinion regarding budgetary deficits and growth of the federal debt, and the fact that public discontent with unemployment of 5 per cent or more for so long was no greater than it was—all these considerations suggest that, in the collective judgment of American policy makers, social welfare was being maximized at an unemployment rate of more than 4 per cent.

It can fairly be stated that the success of the 1964 tax cut has brought about a significant change. There has been a noticeable decline in the degree of concern over budgetary deficits and a greater willingness, by Congress and conservative public opinion, to accept an expansionary fiscal policy. As a result, there has been some shift in the collective welfare function that shapes economic policy. Marginal rates of substitution have altered, so that today a decline in unemployment achieved through fiscal action is thought to entail a lower social cost than it would have a few years ago. As a result, the actual employment goal in the United States today, as it manifests itself in the interaction between the Administration and the Congress, is closer to 4 per cent than it had been when this figure was explicitly put forward at the beginning of the Kennedy Administration.

This greater willingness to use fiscal policy to reduce the level of unemployment can be expressed in terms of the social welfare function presented in Chapter 2. Instead of writing merely

$$Z = f(u, \dot{Y}, \dot{P})$$

subject to the various constraints that we listed, we can expand the welfare function by including one or more fiscal variables. For example, we might write

$$Z = F(u, \dot{Y}, \dot{P}, \dot{G}, D)$$

where $\dot{G}$ is the rate of change in nondefense government expenditures and D is the size of the federal deficit. To the majority of Americans, including Congressmen, social welfare presumably declines with a rise in nondefense federal spending (even if matched by an increase in tax receipts) and also declines with an increase in the federal deficit. These inverse relationships, although continuing to exist in the minds of most Americans after the 1964 tax cut, played a somewhat less important role than they did in earlier years. To say that there was greater acceptance of the New Economics after 1964 is to say that public opinion and the Congress became more willing to accept some increase in the deficit in order to bring about a reduction in unemployment. The resistance to accelerating the rise in federal nondefense expenditures was, and still is, however, quite strong. Thus we note that the expansionary fiscal measures in 1964–1965 took the form primarily of tax reductions rather than large increases in federal nondefense expenditures.

The Kinds of Unemployment

Let us now closely inspect the numbers that we have been citing and take a more intensive look at what is involved in establishing an employment goal as a guide to economic policy. We must examine two sets of issues in particular. One involves the fact that there is more than one kind of unemployment;

the other is concerned with a matter of definition. How shall
the goal of full employment be defined? In particular, how shall
it be defined so as to provide the most helpful guide to economic
policy?

The fact that there are different kinds of unemployment is
important here, because all these different kinds neither result
from the same causes nor respond to the same policy measures.
There is fairly general agreement that, in differentiating among
the causes of unemployment, three sets of factors in particular
must be distinguished.[39] In addition, we shall refer to two other
kinds of unemployment which do not usually enter into discussions of how the goal of full employment should be formulated.

Frictional unemployment. Even with a homogeneous labor force
and a satisfactory level of aggregate demand (we shall return
later to the question as to what constitutes a satisfactory level
in this context), movement to a new job takes time. Hence,
under the best of circumstances, there will be a minimum "float"
of workers in the process of moving to new jobs. This is usually
referred to as "minimum frictional unemployment." Such frictional unemployment is assumed to be balanced by an equal
or larger number of job vacancies. If the labor force is not per-
fectly homogeneous, this frictional minimum may be different
for different segments of the working population.

Seasonal unemployment is frequently included in this notion
of frictional unemployment. Even if seasonal workers withdraw
from the labor force or find other work in the off season, the
frictions and time involved in such movements create a seasonal
pattern in total unemployment. The seasonal pattern of unemployment does not remain constant over the years; and it is
related, in ways which are still not well understood, to changes
in the level of aggregate demand.

Unemployment due to deficient aggregate demand. We may
next list the set of factors implied by what was formerly called
"cyclical" and is now frequently termed "deficiency-of-demand"
unemployment. Implied here is the fact that the *total* demand
for goods and services, with given wage rates and labor productivity, is not sufficient to generate jobs for all those who want
to work (after appropriate adjustment for minimum frictional
unemployment). An implied corollary is that the number of job

vacancies open in the economy as a whole is significantly less
than the total number of people seeking work. This is the kind
of unemployment that rises sharply when a business recession
occurs. It is to the prevention of this type of unemployment
in particular that aggregative full employment policies are addressed. The expansionary fiscal policy followed in the United
States in 1964–1965 was predicated on the assumption that the
excess of current unemployment over the target rate of 4 per
cent was primarily of this deficient-demand variety.

Structural unemployment. The third set of factors is the one
with which the term "structural" unemployment is most frequently associated. Although this term has been used in different
ways, the notion of structural unemployment clearly implies that
two essential conditions prevail in one or more sectors of the
national labor market.[40]

First, *there must be some degree of labor immobility along
one or more dimensions of the labor force.* Thus, even when
there is no deficiency of aggregate demand, there will be particular sectors of the labor force from which workers cannot easily
and quickly move to other sectors in search of jobs. The reasons for such immobility may be many—lack of education or
training, attachment to a community or region, lack of information as to where jobs are available, restrictions on entry into
an occupation, restrictive hiring practices including discrmina-
tion on the basis of race, sex, or religion, and so on.

Second, *in some or all of these sectors with impaired mobility,
unemployment significantly exceeds available vacancies even
when there is no deficiency of aggregate demand.*[41] Supply exceeds demand, at prevailing wage rates, in some sectors of the
labor market, and market forces are not strong enough to eliminate these imbalances where they exist. Hence unemployment
rates are higher in these sectors than in the economy as a whole,
and such differentially high unemployment rates tend to persist
for relatively long periods. The persistence of these differentially
high unemployment rates even at aggregative full employment
means that the imbalance between demand and supply in some
sectors of the labor market is not being removed by either (1)
adjustments in wages, (2) reductions of supply through labor
mobility outward from these sectors, or (3) an increase in de-

mand for the types of labor that have been in excess supply (for example, through revision of employers' hiring standards and practices or the movement of industry into a depressed area).

There may be an imbalance between the demand for and supply of particular kinds of labor for a number of reasons. Three in particular might be cited. First, the demand for particular skills may be reduced because of technological change or a shift in the pattern of demand for output (for example, from goods to services). Discussions of "structural unemployment" in the United States in recent years have emphasized this factor particularly. Second, there may be a shift of economic activity out of a geographical region not matched by a comparable exodus of workers. This leads to the problem of "depressed areas." And third, there may be an influx of workers—of a particular type or into a particular region—at such a rate that they cannot be quickly absorbed into jobs. Thus, the accelerated migration from farm to city of poorly educated workers, particularly Negroes, has helped to create a problem of "structural unemployment" in our urban centers. The rapid increase in the number of teen-agers entering the labor market has had a similar effect. Or to cite a European example, the influx of refugees into West Germany after World War II led to considerable debate regarding the size of the "structural unemployment" problem in that country.

The three sources of structural unemployment cited in the preceding paragraph are all related to identifiable shifts in the pattern of demand for or supply of labor; these are changes to which the economy finds it difficult to adjust because of some degree of labor immobility and wage inflexibility. It is also possible that demand for the supply of a particular kind of labor may have been out of balance as far back as our records go. Immobility, however it came to exist, may perpetuate such sectoral imbalances and create differentially high unemployment rates that continue indefinitely. Such more or less permanent immobility may be associated with a variety of institutional factors. Thus, we expect to find that unemployment rates are higher among the least skilled and educated. We should also expect that unemployment rates would be higher at the extremes of the age distribution than in the prime working ages. And, in the United States, we have the persistent phenomenon of higher unemployment rates among Negroes than among whites.

These structural differentials will be the more marked the more heterogeneous is the labor force—and the measure of heterogeneity in this context is intersectoral immobility. These unemployment differentials are more marked, and the labor force is more heterogeneous, in the United States than in the advanced economies of Western Europe.

These differentially high unemployment rates may contain a frictional as well as a deficient-demand element. Among construction workers, for example, there may be ample vacancies, but the element of weather plus the need to move from job to job will cause frictional unemployment to be higher than in most other industries. Over and above such differentially high frictional unemployment, there may also be a shortage of jobs in relation to supply of this particular kind of labor.

It might be added that it is not easy, in fact, to differentiate between unemployment due to an economy-wide deficiency of demand and that due to structural factors in the sense previously defined.[42] One reason is that variations in aggregate demand affect different groups differently. Another, even the most persistent structural causes of differential employment opportunities tend to weaken in very tight labor markets. The extreme labor tightness in World War II illustrates this. Or, to cite another example, the "structural unemployment" resulting from the influx of refugees into Western Germany largely disappeared in the very tight labor market of the late 1950's and early 1960's.[43]

"Disguised" unemployment. The kinds of unemployment thus far listed describe the situations of persons who are in the labor market and actively seeking jobs. This is the recorded unemployment which the official statistics seek to measure, and it is to such recorded unemployment that the target numbers—2 or 3 or 4 per cent—are presumed to apply.

There has been growing recognition in the United States in the last decade that we must also pay attention to "disguised unemployment"—to those who are not currently seeking work because they believe no jobs are available, but would enter the labor force if employment conditions were to improve.[44] In short, the labor force is sensitive to the level of employment. If aggregate demand declines, the rise in recorded unemployment may be deceptively small, because some of those who lose their jobs may withdraw from the labor market and not be counted as unemployed. Similarly, persons who were about to enter the labor market may defer doing so because of the scarcity of jobs, again holding down the number who are recorded as being unemployed.

Conversely, when employment conditions improve, the decline in recorded unemployment may be much less than the increase in employment as the labor force responds sensitively to the improvement in employment conditions. The labor force increases not only because of demographic and other long-run factors—the increase in population of working age and, for example, an underlying trend for more married women to take part-time or full-time jobs outside the home—but also because persons marginally attached to the labor force enter (ore reenter) the labor market when jobs become easier to obtain.

One way of describing this situation is to say that labor-force participation rates among various segments of the population are sensitive to short-run changes in employment conditions. This is particularly true of married women, those under 25 (particularly teen-agers), and older persons.

Estimates of the amount of disguised unemployment in the United States in recent years have varied widely. In December 1964, when the seasonally adjusted unemployment rate was 5 per cent, it was officially estimated that possibly a million additional persons would enter the labor force if the unemployment rate were brought down to 4 per cent.[45] This implies that disguised unemployment was about 1.3 per cent of the labor force when the recorded unemployment rate was 5 per cent. Other estimates suggest that in recent years disguised unemployment may have been relatively even more important than this estimate implies.[46]

To what extent should our employment goal take account of such disguised unemployment? Even when recorded unemployment is at 4 per cent in the United States, presumably there are still additional persons on the margin of the labor force who would begin to seek jobs if unemployment fell to 3.5 or 3 per cent of the labor force.[47]

At this point, another issue enters arising out of the fact that the disguised unemployed are primarily "secondary" workers—married women and the young and the old. Most are not primary breadwinners, and most have alternatives available outside the labor market (home and school) which become more attractive relatively as recorded unemployment rises and jobs are harder to find. Is the loss in social welfare resulting from a given rise in disguised unemployment of secondary workers as great as it is for the same increase in recorded unemployment of primary workers? For most of us the answer is presumably in the negative. At the same time, however, virtually all would agree that there *is* a decline in welfare when disguised unemployment rises—both because of the loss of potential output and because of the decline in alternatives available to those who retire from the labor market.

How shall the goal of full employment be defined—and quantified—if disguised unemployment is taken into account? Conceptually the problem is simple if we can assume that disguised unemployment declines with recorded unemployment. As recorded unemployment falls, welfare rises because of the decline in *both* kinds of unemployment. For a given decline in recorded unemployment, welfare will rise more rapidly if both types of unemployment are taken into account than if only recorded unemployment is considered. This should lead to maximizing our social welfare function at a lower rate for recorded unemployment than would be the case if the phenomenon of disguised unemployment were ignored. Thus we can continue to express the employment target in terms of recorded unemployment, and we can adjust the target to reflect (1) rough estimates as to how disguised unemployment varies with recorded unemployment and (2) the amount by which we choose to discount the loss of welfare from disguised unemployment because it is composed principally of secondary workers. If our employment goal were a 4 per cent unemployment rate when disguised unemployment was ignored, it should be something less than 4 per cent when the sensitivity of the labor force to employment conditions is taken into account.

Involuntary part-time unemployment. Similar considerations hold for involuntary part-time unemployment, for which we do have rough estimates for the United States. In the calculation of the official unemployment rate, a worker who can find only a part-time job is excluded as completely as one who is working full time. Estimates of labor-force time lost through involuntary part-time as well as total unemployment are presented in Table 1.1. Thus in 1965, when the rate for total unemployment was 4.6 per cent, the percentage of labor time lost through both complete and involuntary part-time unemployment was estimated at 5.0 per cent.

Here, again, we can follow the procedure suggested in the case of disguised unemployment. Explicit consideration of part-time unemployment should lead us to associate a larger contribution to welfare with a given decline in full-time employment than would be present if such part-time unemployment were neglected.

The Next Steps

Thus far we have said merely that aggregative full employment "corresponds to the lowest level to which it is considered *feasible* to reduce the overall unemployment rate," given the amount of frictional and structural unemployment. It is time now to investigate two important questions suggested by this overly elliptical definition.

First, how is "feasible" to be defined in this context, particularly when not only unemployment but also the other variables and constraints in our welfare function are taken into account? And second, what are the implications of adding a structural dimension to the goal of full employment, so that full employment is defined in structural as well as aggregative terms?

These are the questions that we shall consider in Chapter 4.

NOTES

1. For a wide collection of readings on the evolution of employment policy in the United States, see Subcommittee on Employment and Manpower of the Senate Committee on Labor and Public Welfare, *Selected Readings in Employment and Manpower*, 89th Congress, 2nd Session (Washington, D.C.: Government Printing Office, 1965–66), Vols. 5, 6, and 7. These volumes of *Selected Readings* bear the title *History of Employment and Manpower Policy in the United States*.

2. Stephen K. Bailey, *Congress Makes a Law* (New York: Columbia University Press, 1950), p. 5. The discussion which follows owes a great deal to Bailey's valuable study.

3. Quoted in Bailey, *op. cit.*, p. 6. For the full report of the conference, see *Report of the President's Conference on Unemployment* (Washington, D.C.: Government Printing Office, 1921). President Harding's speech appears on pp. 25–28 of the *Report*.

4. *Report of the President's Conference on Unemployment*, p. 29.

5. Republished with a new Part II (London: Longmans, Green and Company, 1930).

6. In addition to the *Report* of the 1921 conference already cited, see *Business Cycles and Unemployment: Report and Recommendations of a Committee of the President's Conference on Unemployment* (New York: McGraw-Hill, 1923); also Herman Feldman, *The Regularization of Employment* (New York: Harper, 1925).

7. William H. Beveridge, *Full Employment in a Free Society* (New York: Norton, 1945, pp. 134–135. (The original British edition was published in 1944.)

8. The most reliable estimates of unemployment for the period before World War II are those of Stanley Lebergott. See his *Manpower in Economic Growth* (New York: McGraw-Hill, 1964), p. 512.

9. For a description of the 1931 act and its implementation, see U.S. Senate, *History of the Employment Stabilization Act of 1931: Report to the Committee on Banking and Currency*, Senate Committee Print No. 3, 79th Congress, 1st Session (Washington: Government Printing Office, 1945). The 1932 act made 300 million dollars available to states and local subdivisions, in the form of advances and loans for relief and work relief projects. Repayment was waived in 1934. See National Resources Planning Board, *Security, Work, and Relief Policies* (Washington: Government Printing Office, 1942), p. 30 and Appendix 2.

10. The agencies referred to are, in order: Civilian Conservation Corps, Federal Emergency Relief Administration, Public Works Administration, Civil Works Administration, Work Projects Administration, and National Recovery Administration.

11. Swedish economists had been debating these and related issues from the beginning of the 1930's, and this debate had a significant influence on Swedish economic policy. See Erik Lundberg, *Business Cycles and Economic Policy* (Cambridge Massachusetts: Harvard University Press, 1957), especially Chap. V.

12. See United Nations, *National and International Measures for Full Employment* (Lake Success, New York: United Nations, 1949).

13. See Bailey, *op. cit.*, Chap. 2; E. G. Nourse, *Economics in the Public Service* (New York: Harcourt, Brace and World, 1953), Chap. 4; also Senate Subcommittee on Employment and Manpower, *op. cit.*, Vol. 6.

14. Bailey, *op. cit.*, pp. 41–42.

15. Section 2 of the Act.

16. See, for example, A. H. Hansen, *Economic Policy and Full Employ-*

ment (New York: McGraw-Hill, 1947); S. E. Harris, *Economic Planning* (New York: Knopf, 1949).

17. Few countries have enacted formal legislation of the sort represented by the American Employment Act of 1946. To cite an early United Nations report: "Commitments to a policy of full employment are . . . contained in various Government declarations, in formal statements of policy published in the form of official documents, and in legislative enactments. In the United Kingdom, Canada and Australia, the employment policies of the Governments are stated in White Papers presented by command to Parliaments. In New Zealand and the United States, employment policies are embodied in Employment Acts." *Maintenance of Full Employment* (Lake Success, N.Y.: United Nations, 1949), p. 9. See also "National Action to Promote Full Employment," *International Labor Review,* **LIX** (June 1949), 684–698. For an interesting account of the circumstances leading to the Canadian White Paper in 1945, see the reminiscent report by the Paper's principal author, W. A. Mackintosh, in S. F. Kaliski (ed.), *Canadian Economic Policy since the War* (Ottawa: Canadian Trade Committee, 1966), Chap. 1.

18. Cmd. 6527 (London: HMSO, 1944), p. 3.

19. Beveridge, *Full Employment* . . . , p. 260. Beveridge did not exaggerate. A later historian of British economic policy after the war could say of the political and economic climate at the beginning of the 1950's: "Conservative governments, no less clearly than Labour governments before them, in fact put full employment first as the main object of policy." J. C. R. Dow, *The Management of the British Economy, 1945–1960* (Cambridge, England: Cambridge University Press, 1964), p. 70.

20. See the convenient summary in Beveridge, *Full Employment* . . . , Part I.

21. *Ibid.,* p. 36.

22. For a useful review of postwar economic policies in Western Europe as well as the United States, see the three volumes of E. S. Kirschen et al., *Economic Policy in Our Time* (Chicago: Rand McNally, 1964).

23. Definitions of frictional and structural unemployment are offered later.

24. In Europe, we frequently encounter the triad 2-2-4, signifying goals of 2 per cent unemployment, increase in the price level not exceeding 2 per cent, and 4 per cent rate of growth in GNP.

25. Thus, "while most governments have accepted the obligation to make the achievement of a high level of employment one of the aims of economic policy, the majority of them do not want this aim to be expressed in any rigid formula embodying an obligation to keep unemployment below a clearly defined level." *International Labor Review,* **LXXIV** (July 1956), 2. UNESCO has regularly asked member countries for the submission of quantitative standards, but few have been offered. One was offered by the United Kingdom, which "replied in 1951 that it had adopted a standard of 3 per cent although it hoped to maintain unemployment at 2 per cent. It had put the standard at 3 per cent, however,

in order to make allowances for unfavourable repercussions on employment that might arise from adverse development in foreign trade." *Ibid.*, p. 3. See also Robert E. Asher et al., *The United Nations and Economic and Social Co-operation* (Washington: The Brookings Institution, 1957), p. 257.

26. Except for the case of Germany, the adjusted unemployment rates for 1959–1964 presented in Table 1.3 fall within the ranges shown here (with two or three exceptions in individual years). Unemployment in Germany in the first half of the 1960's was well below the level correspond‐ing to aggregative full employment.

27. The unemployment rates shown in Table 1.3 have already been standardized to a modest extent by the OECD. The upward adjustment factor needed to make the original official measures comparable to the American standards seems to be about 100 per cent for France and some‐thing less than this for Britain. See the source cited in Note *b* of Table 1.3. In this context, Sir William Beveridge was certainly correct when he said that his proposed target of 3 per cent was conservative rather than "unduly hopeful." (*Full Employment . . .*, p. 128.) By American definitions, his target for Britain was presumably an overall unemployment rate in excess of 4 per cent.

28. Most governments would agree with the view expressed by Arthur F. Burns that "any numerical goal of full employment, once it has been made official, can be easily misinterpreted and become an obstacle to rational economic policy in a changing world." Arthur F. Burns, "Eco‐nomics and Our Public Policy of Full Employment," in Edgar O. Edwards (ed.), *The Nation's Economic Objectives* (Chicago: University of Chicago Press, 1964), p. 64.

29. For further background on the subject of this section, see Joint Economic Committee, *Twentieth Anniversary of the Employment Act of 1946: An Economic Symposium*, 89th Congress, 2nd Session (Washing‐ton: Government Printing Office, 1966).

30. *Economic Report of the President*, January 1947, p. 1. This would have been about 4.3 per cent on the basis of the definitions now in use.

31. *Economic Report of the President*, January 1948, p. 2. See also the report for January 1951, p. 22, where 3.6 per cent was again referred to as "near a practical minimum."

32. *Economic Report of the President*, January 1956, p. 28.

33. The official resistance to explicitly quantifying the employment target was well expressed in the following statement by Arthur Burns to the Joint Economic Committee in January 1955: ". . . although 4 percent of the labor force is nowadays widely regarded as an approximate measure of the average amount of frictional and seasonal unemployment, the Council has not favored this or any other rigid figure to serve as a trigger to governmental action or as a measure of good performance." *Economic Report of the President: Hearings*, 84th Congress, 1st Session (Washington: Government Printing Office, 1955), p. 45.

34. It is interesting, here, to contrast the wording, general tone, and points of emphasis in two successive *Economics Reports of the President*—that of January 1961 (the last one of the Eisenhower Administration) and that of January 1962 (the first of the Kennedy Administration). In January 1961 no reference was made to a specific unemployment target, and heavy emphasis was put on minimizing government intervention, protecting and facilitating private enterprise, and the importance of price stability. The January 1962 *Report* put heavy emphasis on the Federal Government's responsibility, under the Employment Act, to achieve "maximum employment" and explicitly set out a 4 per cent unemployment rate as an interim target. It seems fair to say that the January 1961 *Economic Report* implied an employment goal that yielded a higher unemployment rate than the 4 per cent specified in the January 1962 *Report*. Perhaps more accurately, the earlier *Report* implied not a single figure but a range for the national unemployment rate, with the midpoint of this range being higher than 4 per cent.

35. This is not to suggest that the problem of structural unemployment has been ignored. Indeed, the recent *Economic Reports of the President* have placed increasing emphasis on the problem of structural unemployment, although they have continued to insist that structural factors were not a bar to bringing unemployment down to 4 per cent through monetary-fiscal policies aimed at raising aggregate demand.

36. In addition to the *Economic Report of the President,* January, 1962, see Walter Heller's testimony in *January 1961 Economic Report of the President and The Economic Situation and Outlook,* Hearings before the Joint Economic Committee, 87th Congress, 1st Session (Washington: Government Printing Office, 1961), pp. 325–326, 564.

37. *Economic Report of the President,* January 1962, p. 46.

38. Subcommittee on Employment and Manpower of the Senate Committee on Labor and Public Welfare, *Toward Full Employment: Proposals for a Comprehensive Employment and Manpower Policy in the United States,* 88th Congress, 2nd Session (Washington: Government Printing Office, 1964), p. 40.

39. For other classifications of unemployment, largely along the same lines, see Subcommittee on Economic Statistics of the Joint Economic Committee, *Unemployment: Terminology, Measurement, and Analysis,* 87th Congress, 1st Session (Washington: Government Printing Office, 1961); Bureau of Labor Statistics, *The Extent and Nature of Frictional Unemployment,* Study Paper No. 6 in Joint Economic Committee, *Study of Employment, Growth, and Price Levels,* 86th Congress, 1st Session (Washington: Government Printing Office, 1959); *Report of the Special Committee on Unemployment Problems,* Senate Report No. 1206, 86th Congress, 2nd Session (Washington: Government Printing Office, 1960).

40. For samples of other definitions or less formal attempts to identify structural unemployment, see the essays by Barbara Berman and R. G. Lipsey in A. M. Ross (ed.), *Employment Policy and the Labor Market* (Berkeley: University of California Press, 1965); Eleanor Gilpatrick, *Struc-*

tural Unemployment and Aggregate Demand (Baltimore: The Johns Hopkins Press, 1966), Chap. 1; Albert Rees, in American Bankers Association, *Proceedings of a Symposium on Unemployment* (1964), pp. 21 ff. Interestingly, the widely cited Knowles-Kalichek paper refuses to define structural unemployment on the grounds that the "concept of structural unemployment as applied to particular workers or groups of workers is theoretically meaningless and defies empirical measurement." Instead it speaks of "a rise in unemployment due to structural changes" (or "structural transformation") and seeks to identify and measure the "accompanying symptoms" of a rise in unemployment due to structural changes. See Subcommittee on Economic Statistics of the Joint Economic Committee, *Higher Unemployment Rates, 1957–60: Structural Transformation or Inadequate Demand,* 87th Congress, 1st Session (Washington: Government Printing Office, 1961), p. 7.

41. This implies that there are other sectors in which vacancies exceed unemployment. See Fig. 4.5 and the accompanying discussion in Chapter 4.

42. This is a subject on which there is by now a considerable literature. See in particular the excellent paper by R. G. Lipsey, "Structural and Deficient-Demand Unemployment Reconsidered," in Ross (ed.), *op. cit.,* pp. 210–255.

43. The German experience has been carefully studied by Günter Wittich in an unpublished doctoral dissertation, *The German Road to Full Employment* (Berkeley: University of California, 1966).

44. For an excellent critical evaluation of the evidence on this subject, together with references to the literature, see Jacob Mincer "Labor-Force Participation and Unemployment: A Review of Recent Evidence," in R. A. Gordon and Margaret S. Gordon (eds.), *Prosperity and Unemployment* (New York: John Wiley and Sons, 1966). See also the more recent article by T. F. Dernburg and K. T. Strand, "Hidden Unemployment 1953–62: A Quantitative Analysis by Age and Sex," *American Economic Review,* LVI (March 1966), 71–95.

45. *Economic Report of the President,* January 1965, p. 7.

46. Some other estimates are cited in Note 15 in Chapter 1.

47. The amount of disguised unemployment existing at any time is altogether a relative matter—relative to the level of demand for labor (as measured, say, by the rate of recorded unemployment) which we take as a standard. Obviously, the amount by which the labor force increases within a given period would be larger if the unemployment rate fell to 3 per cent than if it fell just to 4 per cent. Most estimates of disguised unemployment in the United States use as a standard a rate for recorded unemployment of 4 per cent. For an attempt to measure disguised unemployment for the period 1953–1962 relative to full employment standards of both 4 and 3 per cent, see K. T. Strand and T. F. Dernburg, "Cyclical Variation in Civilian Labor Force Participation," *Review of Economics and Statistics,* XLVI (November 1964), 385–388. There are reasons to believe that their estimates of disguised unemployment are too high. See Mincer, *op. cit.*

CHAPTER 4

Aggregative and Structural Full Employment

We have thus far defined aggregative full employment simply as the lowest level to which it is "feasible" to reduce the overall unemployment rate—given both the amount of minimum frictional (including seasonal) unemployment and also the structural factors which make some sectors of the labor force more vulnerable to unemployment than others. This definition takes the amount of frictional and structural unemployment as given.[1] If our aggregative employment goal is 4 per cent, then presumably frictional and structural unemployment add up to 4 per cent. If the current unemployment rate is, in fact, 5 per cent, the excess of 1 per cent over the employment target is attributed to a deficiency of aggregate demand.

Essentially this same definition of the full employment target was proposed shortly after the war by a group of experts appointed by the United Nations. As they put it:[2]

> In industrialized countries, targets should be defined in terms of unemployment rather than employment, and they should be expressed in terms of the smallest percentage of unemployment of wage-earners which the country can *reasonably hope to maintain* in the light of seasonal movements and in the light of structural changes in the economy, which inevitably give rise to some temporary unemployment that could not be eliminated through public policy.

Let us note two points about this definition, which has had widespread acceptance. First, it concerns itself only with *aggregative* full employment. The structural dimensions of the problem are taken as given.[3] The second point to be noted concerns the words in the definition that we have italicized. Full employment is to be defined in terms of the lowest unemployment rate which a country can "reasonably hope to maintain." This is the counterpart of the phrase in our own definition: the lowest level to which it is "feasible" to reduce the overall unemployment rate. What is to be our criterion of feasibility? What determines the lowest percentage to which we can "reasonably hope" to reduce unemployment through measures aimed at the level of aggregate demand?[4]

Full Employment and the Welfare Function

We suggested an answer to this question in Chapter 2. Social welfare is a function of the various aggregative target variables, subject to certain constraints related to the balance of payments. We wrote the welfare function as

$$Z = f(u, \dot{Y}, \dot{P})$$

subject to a list of constraints. Social welfare is assumed to be inversely related to the unemployment rate (u) and the rate of change in prices $(\dot{P})$ and positively related to the rate of growth in output $(\dot{Y})$. The goal of the policy maker is to seek to achieve that unemployment rate—given the way unemployment is related to both the other target variables and the constraints listed in Chapter 2—which will, given his value judgments, maximize social welfare.[5]

This, of course, immediately raises the question as to how unemployment is related to the other target variables. Let us consider first the relation between the level of unemployment and the rate of growth of output. Certainly, a *decline* in unemployment will be associated with an accelerated expansion in output—as long as unemployment is falling. But is a low, unchanging rate of unemployment (say, 3 per cent in the United States) likely to be associated with a slower or faster rate of growth in total output than a higher unemployment rate (say, 4 or 5 per cent)? On the whole, the evidence points to an inverse relationship. Above some minimum unemployment rate, growth is likely to be faster at a lower than at a higher unemployment rate.[6] Certainly the relationship is not a simple one, and much depends on a variety of conditioning factors which are here taken as given.[7] But it would appear that, as a first approximation, we can consider full employment and rapid growth as complementary and not as competing goals.[8]

The opposite is true of the relation between unemployment and the rate of change in prices. Here, there does seem to be an inverse relationship. The lower the level of unemployment (and the faster unemployment falls) the greater is likely to be the rise in prices. Thus we must balance the gain in welfare from reducing the level of unemployment against the loss in welfare which is associated with the accelerated rise in prices that may result. An accelerated rise in prices may have a twofold effect on welfare. A rise (or fall) in prices is assumed in and of itself to detract from welfare. In addition, an accelerated rise in prices, depending on what is happening to prices abroad, may bring into operation the balance-of-payments constraint, in the manner described in Chapter 2.[9]

Full Employment and Price Stability

These considerations suggest a simplification of our welfare function which has been widely accepted as a basis for formulating the full-employment goal. Since we have concluded that growth and full employment are, on the whole, complementary goals, we may simplify our welfare function by omitting $\dot{Y}$ and write

$$Z = f(u, \dot{P})$$

where welfare is inversely related to both the unemployment rate and the rate of change in prices. Each of the two variables in the parentheses affects welfare not only directly but also through its association with other variables or constraints.

Given this simplified welfare function, we can then define the full employment target as that unemployment rate which will maximize welfare when allowance is made for the welfare effects of the rate of change in the price level which is associated with that level of unemployment.[10]

These relationships can be illustrated in Fig. 4.1, which is based on a similar formulation by Richard Lipsey.[11] The curve XX', which is a variant of what has come to be called the "Phillips curve," portrays the relationship which is assumed to hold between the unemployment rate (horizontal axis) and the rate of change in prices (vertical axis). The lower unemployment drops, the faster prices rise. Only at an unemployment rate of Oe is the price level constant. This curve is drawn on the assumption that there is a given amount of frictional-structural-unemployment.

The curves which are concave to the origin are indifference curves reflecting the policy maker's "marginal rates of substitution" between a little less unemployment and a slightly faster rise in prices. Each of the indifference curves represents a different

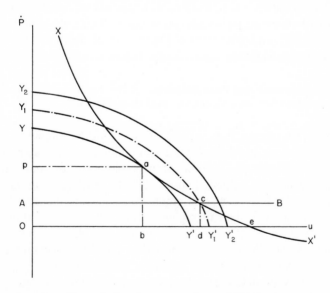

Fig. 4.1. The relation between price stability and unemployment.

level of welfare; welfare increases as the indifference curves move southwest toward the origin. The curve Y_2Y_2' represents a lower level of welfare than Y_1Y_1', whereas YY' represents a higher level of welfare than does Y_1Y_1'.

Let us assume for a moment than no balance-of-payments constraint is in operation.[12] Then, given the relationship between unemployment and inflation denoted by the curve XX', the policy maker will seek to reach the point a, where his indifference curve is tangent to XX'. Given XX', this maximizes economic welfare as he conceives it, with an unemployment rate Ob and a rate of price increase equal to Op. Thus Ob is his target for aggregative full employment.

What happens if we explicitly introduce a balance-of-payments constraint? Let us say that OA is the maximum rate of increase in the domestic price level that is permissible if balance-of-payments equilibrium is to be maintained. The line AB cuts the XX' curve at c, which corresponds to an unemployment rate of Od. One can say that the policy maker has been forced to operate on the truncated indifference curve AcY_1'. The section cY_1' is part of the curve Y_1cY_1' (which would exist in the absence of the balance-of-payments constraint). This curve is to the right of YY' and represents a lower level of welfare, as viewed by the policy maker.

The Relation Between Vacancies and Unemployment

Since the publication of Beveridge's *Full Employment in a Free Society*, it has been common to define the full employment goal by relating the volume of unemployment to the number of job vacancies rather than to the attendant rate of change in prices. To Beveridge, full employment meant "having always more vacant jobs than unemployed men." This formulation has generally been criticized as going too far, and the criterion today is usually merely stated in terms of an equality between vacancies and unemployment.[13]

This way of defining full employment is illustrated in graph A of Fig. 4.2. The vacancy rate is measured on the vertical axis, the unemployment rate on the horizontal.[14] The 45-degree

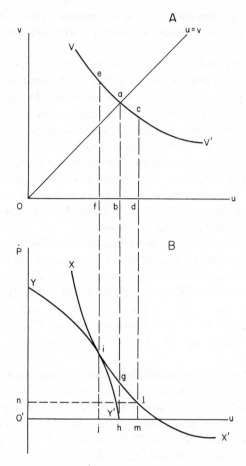

Fig. 4.2. The relations (A) between vacancies and unemployment and (B) between price stability and unemployment.

line portrays all possible situations that correspond to an equality of vacancies and unemployment. The curve VV' represents the relation assumed to exist between vacancies and unemployment as aggregate demand varies, given the factors determining the amount of frictional and structural unemployment. Point

a represents a situation in which vacancies equal unemployment—that is, full employment—at an unemployment rate of
Ob.

How does this relate to the price-stability criterion illustrated
in Fig. 4.1? To show the relationship, let us examine graph *B*
of Fig. 4.2. Here, the vertical scale measures the rate of price
change, as in Fig 4.1. On the horizontal axis we have the rate
of unemployment, using the same scale as in graph A. The curve
XX' shows the rate of price change associated with each possible
level of unemployment. When vacancies equal unemployment
at point *a* in graph *A*, at an unemployment rate of *Ob*, we see
in graph *B* that this unemployment rate has associated with
it a rate of price increase of *gh*.[15] Does this correspond to full
employment by our previous criterion?

The answer is obvious. Not having specified the policy maker's
preference function, we cannot say. Let us assume that the policy
maker does have a set of preference functions like those in Fig.
4.1, and that curve *YY'* in graph *B* of Fig. 4.2 is the one that
is tangent to curve *XX'* at point *i*. Then the full employment
goal corresponds to an unemployment rate of *O'j*, not *O'h*, and
this goal requires (graph *A*) that vacancies be in excess of
unemployment.

Let us take another possibility. Assume that balance-of-payments considerations impose the price constraint represented by
the horizontal line *nl* in graph *B*, so that the policy maker is
forced to accept an unemployment rate of *O'm* (= *Od* in graph
A of Fig. 4.2). This gives us "full employment" with unemployment substantially in excess of vacancies.

This suggests that the relationship between vacancies and unemployment does not provide an adequate basis for defining
the goal of full employment and quantifying the employment
target. In brief, it ignores the other related variables which also
affect welfare. In addition, we should mention the practical difficulties. Reliable vacancy data do not yet exist in the United
States; moreover, serious problems exist both in developing such
data and in interpreting what they mean.[16] In particular, little
confidence can be placed in the specific criterion of an equality
between officially reported vacancies and unemployment. Depending on how vacancies are defined and reported, the number

of vacancies may or may not be approximately equal to the number unemployed in situations generally considered to correspond to full employment.[17]

This does not mean that vacancy data may not provide highly valuable guides in the administration of employment and manpower policy. Such statistics have proved extremely useful in countries that have developed them, and it is highly desirable that the United States have a comprehensive system of reporting job openings, in suitable detail, as soon as possible. However, it is necessary to repeat, a simple comparison of the absolute levels of vacancies and of unemployment does not by itself provide us with an adequate basis for defining and quantifying the goal of full employment.

While the simplified welfare function illustrated in Fig. 4.1 provides a conceptual basis for *defining* the full employment goal, it does not help us very much in arriving at a *quantitative* goal to serve as a guide to policy. Thus far, attempts to verify the precise relation between the level of unemployment and the associated change in prices (or wages) in the United States, particularly for the postwar period, have not met with notable success. Other variables are certainly involved, and the short-run function portrayed by the curve XX' in Fig. 4.1 shifts and changes its shape for reasons that are not yet fully understood.[18] (In addition, as we shall see in the next section, the curve shifts as the volume of frictional and structural unemployment changes.) Furthermore, there is obviously no way of giving quantitative expression to the indifference curves shown in Fig. 4.1.

The setting of a full employment target must therefore continue to be based on very rough-and-ready procedures, in which the changing preference functions of successive policy makers are applied to crude impressions of the (also changing) relationships that are presumed to hold between the level of unemployment and the other relevant variables. In the United States, this crude process has led to the present official "interim target" of an overall unemployment rate of 4 per cent. Outside the White House and the Council of Economic Advisers, differing sets of value judgments and differing views as to the nature of the underlying relationships have led to suggested targets below and above 4 per cent—largely in the range of from 3 to 5 per cent.

Structural as Well as Aggregative Full Employment

Thus far we have been considering only the goal of *aggregative* full employment, in which we took as given the factors determining the amount of frictional and structural unemployment. It is time now to turn to the structural aspects of the problem.

We are beginning increasingly to recognize, on both sides of the Atlantic, that a full-fledged national employment policy must be aimed at something more than just the *overall* rate of unemployment. The pattern of unemployment—among different occupations, regions, age groups, and so on—is also crucially important. If the overall unemployment rate in the United States is 4 per cent, can it be said that we enjoy "full employment" if the unemployment rate at the same time is 8 per cent among Negroes, 10 per cent among white teen-agers, and 20 per cent among Negro teen-agers?

Increasing emphasis on the structural aspects of unemployment has been characteristic of European countries as well as the United States. As overall unemployment has fallen to levels that seem very low by prewar and early postwar standards, European governments have come to place increasing emphasis on the differentially high unemployment rates that remain for particular sectors of the labor force. The labor force throughout Europe is much more homogeneous than that in the United States. There is no color problem;[19] in general, teen-agers are readily absorbed into the ranks of the employed; and there are no particularly marked differentials between average unemployment rates for blue-collar and white-collar workers. Nearly every country, however, does have some variant of a depressed-area problem—more serious in some countries than in others—and in some countries, particularly the United Kingdom, unemployment rates are relatively high among the unskilled.[20]

The development of an integrated labor market policy to deal with such differential unemployment rates—and more generally to expedite the adjustment of labor supply to the changing pattern of labor demand—began earlier and has proceeded further in Europe than the United States. The most fully developed of these programs is that of Sweden, which has probably set its employment target higher than any other country in the West.[21]

The increasing tempo of technological change in Western Europe has reinforced this emphasis on the structural aspects of unemployment. The following statement applying to the situation in France is of interest here:[22]

> For the notion of full employment, elaborated following the war, the development of technical progress requires now substituting that of employment equilibrium, infinitely more delicate to define and put into practice. The labor market, then relatively homogeneous, where problems presented themselves only in quantitative terms and where solutions consisted only in encouraging the fluidity of manpower, now reveals itself differentiated into several markets, bound together, to be sure, by the economic environment, but regulated by their own rules, conditions, and rhythms. Multiplying the risks of structural unemployment, this diversity makes more complex, and at the same time more necessary, public intervention which must henceforth deal with qualitative data.

Emphasis on policies to cope with the structural aspects of unemployment has increased tremendously in the United States in the last few years—witness the Area Redevelopment Act (now the Public Works and Economic Development Act), the greatly enlarged program under the Manpower Development and Training Act, the Economic Opportunity Act, the new program of federal aid to education, the civil rights legislation, and still other measures aimed at improving employment opportunities for the disadvantaged segments of the labor force. Today, the President is required to submit to Congress each year not only an *Economic Report*—concerned largely with our aggregative economic goals, particularly that of aggregative full employment—but also a *Manpower Report*—which deals with the structural aspects of ensuring that all "those able, willing, and seeking to work" can find jobs for which they are qualified.

A diagrammatic representation. What is involved in giving a structural dimension to the goal of full employment can be il-

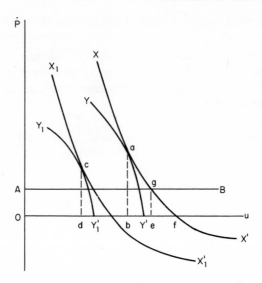

Fig. 4.3. The relation between price stability
and unemployment at different levels of structural unemployment.

lustrated by use of diagrams similar to those we employed in
defining the goal of aggregative full employment.

Figure 4.3, which is similar to Fig. 4.1, illustrates the relationship between unemployment and the rate of change in the price
level under two different sets of conditions with respect to the
severity of structural unemployment. Underlying structural (and
frictional) factors determine the distance of the XX' curves from
the origin and also help to determine the shape of the curves.
Thus the curve XX' portrays a situation with more structural
and frictional unemployment than does X_1X_1'. Under the conditions portrayed by XX', some price increase can be avoided
only at the expense of an unemployment rate equal to Of. If
the policy maker's welfare function implies indifference curves
such as YY', then the aggregative full employment goal will
be set at an unemployment rate of Ob. If the balance of payments imposes the constraint represented by the horizontal line
AB, the full employment target will involve an unemployment
rate of Oe.

Suppose that a successful manpower policy results in reducing the hard core of structural and frictional unemployment so that we move from XX' to X_1X_1'. If the policy maker's preferences are given by Y_1Y_1', the aggregative full employment goal can be set at the lower unemployment rate of Od.

Thus, if we are to have a policy of *both* structural and aggregative full employment, we must ask the following question. By means of the various instruments of manpower policy (training and retraining programs, reduction of discrimination in hiring, an improved employment service, relocation of workers, and the like) how far is a government prepared to go in reducing the amount of unemployment that exists at aggregative full employment? Or, in terms of our diagram, how far is it prepared to go in seeking to shift the XX' curve to the left? The answer to this question, when costs and benefits are weighed on the scales of the policy maker's value system, yields what we may call aggregative *and* structural full employment. In the United States, aggregative full employment has been officially interpreted since 1961 as implying an overall unemployment rate of 4 per cent—the "interim target" of the Council of Economic Advisers. But it is also the official belief—as reflected in the various pieces of manpower legislation—that unemployment can be brought down to a lower figure (3 per cent is the figure most often mentioned) at a cost that is worth incurring in terms of the benefits to be achieved. The benefits are measured less in the decline of the overall rate than in the reduction in unemployment among the groups which now have the highest unemployment rates.

Indeed, as we shall emphasize in Chapter 7, a full-fledged policy of aggregative and structural full employment must have not a single quantitative target but an entire matrix of target figures—target unemployment rates for each of the important sectors of the labor force.[23] As a less satisfactory alternative, the goal might be set in terms of both an overall rate and a measure of dispersion of sectoral unemployment rates around the average represented by the overall rate. We shall consider one possible dispersion measure in Chapters 5 and 6.

The relation between aggregative and structural full employment can also be illustrated by the vacancies–unemployment

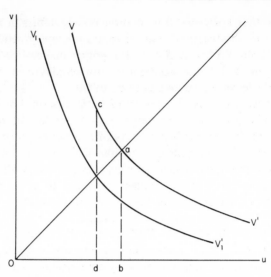

Fig. 4.4. Relation between vacancies and unemployment at different levels of structural unemployment.

relationship indicated in Fig. 4.4, which is similar to graph A of Fig 4.2. VV' represents the relation between the vacancy rate and the unemployment rate under one set of conditions determining the level of structural and frictional unemployment. Here vacancies equal unemployment at an unemployment rate of Ob. If now, manpower policy succeeds in shifting the curve from VV' to V_1V_1', vacancies are equal to unemployment at a lower unemployment rate, Od. As in Fig. 4.3, a successful manpower policy permits us to set a higher goal (a lower overall unemployment rate) for aggregative employment policy.

Figure 4.4. helps to illuminate the character of structural unemployment and the reasons why so many countries have awakened to the need for detailed manpower programs. Let us assume that a country faces labor market conditions exemplified by the curve VV' and seeks to reduce unemployment from, say, Ob to Od merely by expanding aggregate demand. As total spending is increased, vacancies will rise (from ab to cd) more rapidly than unemployment is reduced (from Ob to Od). This results from the fact that many of the unemployed do not have the qualifications, or are not in the right places, for the jobs that open up. And the greater the excess of vacancies over unemployment, presumably, the stronger will be the inflationary forces operating on the economy.

If, however, unemployed workers can be moved and trained or retrained for the new jobs created by expanding demand, so that V_1V_1' rather than VV' comes to represent the state of the labor market, then the lower unemployment rate can be achieved without building up inflationary pressures. Indeed, in this case, vacancies decline *pari passu* with the fall in unemployment—and output increases.

A Cross-Sectional View

In our diagrams and discussion thus far, we have considered the relation between *total* unemployment and the *total* number of job vacancies for alternative levels of aggregate demand. However, there is still another way of considering the relation between vacancies and unemployment. We can look at the vacancies-unemployment relation for each segment of the labor force classified in a particular way—for example, by occupation or region—at a given level of aggregate demand. We can call this the cross-sectional relationship between vacancies and unemployment. A simple illustration is provided by Fig. 4.5.

Here we assume that the labor force is divided into four groups (for example, four broad occupational groups ranging from the most to the least skilled). For a given level of aggregate demand, the vacancy–unemployment relation for each of the four groups is given by the points A, B, C, and D. At A, vacancies are greatly in excess of unemployment; the reverse is true at point D (presumably representing the least skilled). As we have plotted the points, total vacancies for the entire labor force equals total unemployment at point E on the 45-degree line.[24] Thus, using the vacancy–unemployment criterion, we have a situation of aggregate full employment. But labor is in excess supply in two sectors, and there is a labor shortage in the other two. Immobility prevents workers from moving from the sectors of labor surplus to those with a labor shortage.

Suppose that, through an effective manpower program, a given number of the unemployed in each of sectors C and D become qualified for jobs in the labor shortage sectors. We might then get the situation traced out by $A'B'C'D'$. Unemployment is reduced by a given amount, with no change in vacancies, in each of sectors C and D; and vacancies are reduced by the same amount, with no change in unemployment, in each of sectors A and B. The overall unemployment rate falls from Oa to Ob,

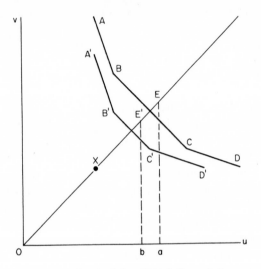

Fig. 4.5. Cross-sectional relation between vacancies and unemployment.

provided that there is an appropriate expansion in aggregate demand in order to absorb the increase in employment and output in sectors A and B.

We can conceive of a wide variety of kinds of shifts that could occur in the cross-sectional vacancies–unemployment relationship. The closer to the 45-degree line manpower policy can squeeze the points A, B, C, D, the lower will structural unemployment be; and, if aggregate demand expands correspondingly, the lower will total unemployment be. If in Fig. 4.5, for example, we assume that minimum frictional unemployment for all sectors can be made as low as the rate of unemployment initially in the tightest labor market (sector A), a transfer of workers from C and D to A and B might conceivably go on (if enough unemployed workers could be successfully matched against vacant jobs) until all four sectors were at point X on the 45-degree line. At this point only minimum frictional unemployment, assumed to be the same for all sectors, would remain.[25]

In actual life, as we noted earlier, we cannot expect frictional

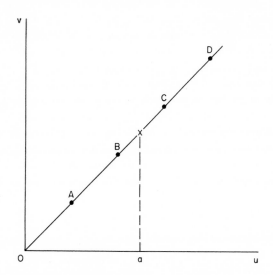

Fig. 4.6. Situation in which vacancies equal unemployment in all sectors but at different levels.

unemployment to be the same for all parts of the labor force. Thus we might have the situation displayed in Fig. 4.6. Here vacancies are equal to unemployment in all of our sectors, A, B, C, and D, but at different levels, so that all of our cross-sectional points fall on the 45-degree line. Vacancies equal unemployment *in toto* and for each sector separately. (The overall unemployment rate is Oa.) Even in this instance, there may still be room for manpower policy to reduce frictional unemployment in those sectors in which it is relatively high.

We would need more evidence before we could characterize

the situation illustrated in Fig. 4.6 as one of full employment, both aggregative and structural. We have not defined full employment in terms of an equality between unemployment and vacancies but in terms of the policy maker's trade-off between lower unemployment and a faster rise in prices. Depending on how vacancies are defined and reported, aggregative full employment in our terms may imply an excess or deficiency of total vacancies in relation to total unemployment.[26] Thus, under conditions of aggregative and structural full employment as we should define this goal, the points A, B, C, and D in Fig. 4.6 might lie along a line above or below the 45-degree line representing an equality of vacancies and unemployment. This would depend on how vacancies are defined and reported. But, if vacancies (and unemployment) are defined and reported similarly in all sections of the labor market, the reported vacancy-unemployment ratio should be roughly the same in all sectors of the labor market if structural as well as aggregative full employment is to exist. The situation should be somewhat as shown in Fig. 4.6 (although not necessarily along the 45-degree line)— and not as seen in Fig. 4.5.

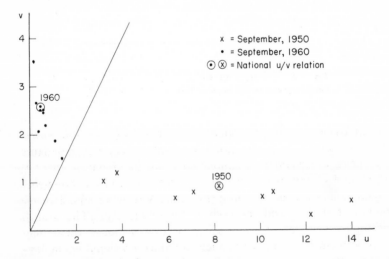

Fig. 4.7. Relation between vacancies and unemployment in West German Länder, 1950 and 1960. (In per cent.)

The cross-sectional relationship between vacancies and unemployment will, of course, shift up and down with changes in the level of aggregate demand. This is nicely illustrated in Fig. 4.7, which displays the vacancy-unemployment relationship in various states (Länder) of West Germany at two different dates: in September 1950, when the national unemployment rate was 8.2 per cent, and in September 1960, when the overall unemployment rate had fallen to as low as 0.5 per cent. The strong movement to the left and upward from 1950 to 1960, as total unemployment fell and vacancies rose, is quite dramatic.[27]

The New Emphasis on Manpower Policy

As we have already noted, interest in the structural aspects of employment policy has grown rapidly in the United States in the last few years. Clearly there has been a shift in welfare functions—in the Administration, in Congress, and among the public at large. This has been perhaps most dramatically demonstrated in the increased concern over inadequate employment opportunities for Negroes. Equally or more important, there has been a growing awareness of changes that have been occurring in the pattern of both the demand for and the supply of labor.

Thus we have witnessed the vigorous debate regarding the extent to which accelerating technological change might be increasing the volume of structural unemployment. There has been growing awareness of the steady shift from blue-collar to white-collar employment and of the growing importance of the service industries. Both the character of technological developments and the changing pattern of demand have dramatically increased the importance of education as a qualification for employment.

On the supply side of the labor market, there have also been important changes. The accelerated inflow of teen-agers into the labor market and the rise in teen-age unemployment have attracted wide attention. Less obvious, but persisting over a longer period, has been the steady increase in the labor-force participation of married women. And finally, involving both the demand and supply sides of the labor market, we have had the accelerated decline in agricultural employment and the marked rise in the urban labor force, the latter being fed by the steady flow of poorly qualified workers from the rural areas.[28]

Although there has been an increased sensitivity to the structural aspects of the general problem of unemployment, and although the American people and the federal government are more committed to a vigorous manpower policy than they were a decade ago, a detailed set of quantified targets to guide policy do not yet exist. We might even argue, with considerable justification, that such detailed targets should not exist. But clearly we need to be more specific than we have been about the relation between particular unemployment rates and the overall rate and about the costs and benefits of programs to reduce specific rates by particular amounts. To cite only one question of considerable importance, is an ultimate goal of 3 per cent for aggregative full employment consistent with the best pattern of particular unemployment rates—by age, color, occupation, or education— that we can hope to achieve through the manpower programs now in operation or likely to be adopted in the years immediately ahead? This is a question to which we shall return in the final chapter.

NOTES

1. It also assumes some particular relationship between registered full-time unemployment, on the one hand, and disguised and involuntary part-time unemployment, on the other.

2. *National and International Measures for Full Employment* (Lake Success: United Nations, 1949), p. 74. Italics added.

3. *Ibid.*, pp. 12–13. The authors of this definition were not unaware of the importance of unemployment resulting from some cause other than a deficiency of demand, and indeed they emphasized the need for labor market policies to reduce frictional and structural unemployment. But they considered such unemployment to be outside the scope of their report.

4. For an earlier discussion of the criteria that might be used to determine the level of unemployment corresponding to full employment, see Albert Rees, "The Meaning and Measurement of Full Employment," in Universities-National Bureau Committee for Economic Research, *The Measurement and Behavior of Unemployment* (Princeton: Princeton University Press, 1957), pp. 13–62.

5. As indicated in Note 15 in Chapter 2, in a complete formulation

we should also have to consider the effect on welfare of the instrument variables (such as taxes) that the policy maker has at his disposal.

6. It may be assumed that there is a lower limit below which still lower levels of unemployment do not contribute to a faster rate of growth, apart from the inflationary and balance-of-payments problems that may be associated with very low unemployment rates. Thus very low unemployment may lead to labor bottlenecks and otherwise retard the rise in labor productivity. It is probable that some Western European countries had reached this point by the mid-1960's.

7. Lower unemployment and more rapid growth are most likely to occur together when both are achieved by expanding aggregate demand. However, if growth is stimulated by measures that operate on the supply side—for example, increasing labor productivity by measures that accelerate technical change—more rapid growth may be associated with a higher level of structural and frictional unemployment. This does not, however, seem to have happened in Western Europe in the postwar period.

8. For some consideration of the relation between the level of unemployment and the growth rate, see the papers by L. R. Klein and R. G. Bodkin and by Tibor and Anne Scitovsky in Commission on Money and Credit, *Inflation, Growth, and Employment* (Englewood Cliffs, New Jersey: Prentice-Hall, 1964); R. G. Bodkin's paper in S. F. Kaliski (ed.), *Canadian Economic Policy Since the War* (Ottawa: Canadian Trade Committee, 1966).

9. See the section on "Price Stability as a Constraint."

10. This is not quite precise. It would be more accurate to say "change in the price level which would result from the policy measures used to bring about a given level of unemployment." The price effects associated with a given level of unemployment will depend in part on the specific measures used to achieve that unemployment level.

11. R. G. Lipsey, "Structural and Deficient-Demand Unemployment Reconsidered," in A. M. Ross (ed.), *Employment Policy and the Labor Market* (Berkeley: University of California Press, 1965), p. 211.

12. This might be true for any of several reasons: (1) the existence of a flexible exchange rate, or (2) a sufficiently rapid rise of prices abroad so that the balance-of-payments constraint on the rate of change in prices does not operate in the relevant range (this was the situation in Germany for a number of years in the postwar period and also in the United States in the early postwar period), or (3) because deficits in the balance of trade are offset by capital imports or foreign aid.

13. For a recent statement, see Arthur F. Burns, "Economics and Our Public Policy of Full Employment," in Edgar O. Edwards (ed.), *The Nation's Economic Objectives* (Chicago: University of Chicago Press, 1964), pp. 65–66. For an earlier statement that full employment should be defined in terms of an equality between vacancies and the number unemployed, see Emile Benoit-Smullyan, "On the Meaning of Full Employment," *Review of Economics and Statistics*, **XXX** (May 1948), 127–134.

For a review of some of the issues involved in this approach, see Rees, *op. cit.*, pp. 36–39.

14. For similar representations of the relation between vacancies and unemployment, see J. C. R. Dow and L. A Dicks-Mireaux, "The Excess Demand for Labour: A Study of Conditions in Great Britain, 1946–1956," *Oxford Economic Papers,* **X** (February 1958), 1–33, and K. J. Hancock, "Unemployment in Australia" in *Labor Problems in the Australian Economy* (University of Adelaide, Eighth Summer School of Business Administration, 1963), pp. 35–54.

15. Note that we have drawn Fig. 4.2 so that an equality of vacancies and unemployment is associated with some increase in the price level. This is a realistic assumption for most countries since World War II. An equality of vacancies and unemployment does *not* automatically imply complete price stability.

16. *The Measurement and Interpretation of Job Vacancies* (New York: National Bureau of Economic Research, 1966).

17. It has been stated that "no country uses a method which provides job vacancy statistics that are substantially complete and fully comparable with a similar complete estimate of unemployment." W. C. Shelton and A. F. Neef, "Foreign Job Vacancy Statistics Programs," in *The Measurement and Interpretation of Job Vacancies,* previously cited, p. 170.

18. See, for example, G. L. Perry, *Unemployment, Money Wage Rates and Inflation* (Cambridge, Massachusetts: M.I.T. Press, 1966) and "The Determinants of Wage Rate Changes and the Inflation-Unemployment Trade-Off for the United States," *Review of Economic Studies,* **XXXI** (October 1964), 287–308; K. B. Griffin, "A Note on Wages, Prices, and Unemployment," *Bulletin of the Oxford Institute of Statistics,* **XXIV** (August 1962), 379–385; W. G. Bowen and R. A. Perry, "Unemployment Conditions and Movements of the Money Wage Level," *Review of Economics and Statistics,* **XLV** (May 1963), 163–172; R. J. Bhatia, "Unemployment and the Rate of Change of Money Earnings in the U.S., 1900–58," *Economica,* **XXVIII** (August 1961), 286–296; P. A. Samuelson and R. M. Solow, "Analytical Aspects of Anti-Inflation Policy," *American Economic Review: Papers and Proceedings,* **L** (May 1960), 177–194; Otto Eckstein and T. A. Wilson, "The Determination of Money Wages in American Industry," *Quarterly Journal of Economics,* **LXXVI** (August 1962), 379–414; and C. L. Schultze and J. L. Tryon, "Prices and Wages," in J. S. Duesenberry et al., *The Brookings Quarterly Econometric Model of the United States* (Chicago: Rand McNally, 1965), pp. 311–333. This sample from the extensive literature on the "Phillips curve" is limited to studies of the relationship between unemployment and wages (or prices) in the United States.

19. Except to a limited extent in the United Kingdom.

20. Differentially high unemployment rates also exist for teen-agers in France and Sweden and for the older age groups in Belgium, Sweden, and the United Kingdom.

21. By way of illustration I cite the following statement by the Director of the Labor Market Board in Sweden: "An active employment policy may be defined as 'measures which affect labour as a factor in production and are so varied, so individualized as—in time—to fit every single person on the employment market.' " The main features of such an employment policy are "geographic mobility of manpower, increased training and retraining and a policy for the location of industry that is well adapted to prevailing conditions." B. Olsson, "Employment Policy in Sweden," *International Labor Review,* **LXXXVII** (May 1963), pp. 411, 413. See also his paper in R. A. Gordon (ed.), *Toward a Manpower Policy* (New York: John Wiley and Sons, 1967).

22. From a statement of M. Gilbert Grandval, Minister of Labor, in the National Assembly during the debate on the National Employment Fund, November 28, 1963, reproduced in *Revue Française du Travail,* **XVII** (October–December 1963), 13.

23. As one advocate has put it, full employment should be defined "in terms of (a) the desired overall employment of our manpower resources and a corresponding minimum overall rate of unemployment, and (b) the desired utilization of our manpower resources by age, sex, color, geography, industry, occupation, and so on, and a correspondingly minimum set of differential unemployment rates." Seymour Wolfbein, "The First Year of the Manpower Act," in Arthur M. Ross (ed.), *Unemployment and the American Economy* (New York: John Wiley and Sons, 1964), p. 56. For similar statements, see John T. Dunlop, "Public Policy and Unemployment," in Special Committee on Unemployment Problems, U.S. Senate, *Studies in Unemployment,* 86th Congress, 2nd Session (Washington: Government Printing Office, 1960), pp. 1–15, and Subcommittee on Employment and Manpower of the Senate Committee on Labor and Public Welfare, *Toward Full Employment: Proposals for a Comprehensive Employment and Manpower Policy in the United States,* 88th Congress, 2nd Session (Washington: Government Printing Office, 1964).

24. As Fig. 4.5 is drawn, we assume that the labor force is evenly distributed among the four sectors.

25. As Fig. 4.5 is drawn, placing the point X directly below A implies more than that the excess vacancies in A and B are filled by the excess unemployed in C and D. This alone would put the point X on the 45-degree line a bit higher than shown. Placing X directly under A implies not only making vacancies equal unemployment in all sectors, but further reducing unemployment and vacancies until they are as low in all other sectors as they are in A. This implies some reduction in total frictional unemployment.

26. It will be remembered that William Beveridge argued that, at least for the British, vacancies should exceed unemployment at full employment.

27. I owe this chart to Günter Wittich. It is from his unpublished doctoral dissertation, *The German Road to Full Employment* (Berkeley:

University of California Library, 1966). The reader should note that the vertical scale for the vacancy rate has been made twice that for the unemployment rate because of the relatively narrow range in which the reported vacancy figures fall. This explains the steepness of the vacancies-equal-unemployment diagonal.

28. For a review of these developments, see R. A. Gordon and Margaret S. Gordon (eds.), *Prosperity and Unemployment* (New York: John Wiley and Sons, 1966).

CHAPTER 5

The Pattern of Unemployment: Some Problems of Measurement

We now begin to examine the actual pattern of unemployment in the United States and also the way in which this pattern has changed since World War II. If the United States is to have a policy of *structural* as well as aggregative full employment, we must, in fact, clearly identify the structural dimensions of the unemployment problem.

More specifically, answers are needed to such questions as those that follow. With what characteristics of the labor force—such as age, sex, occupation, and so on—is the incidence of unemployment associated? What has been the pattern of unemployment with respect to these various characteristics? How have these patterns changed in recent years, and why? And, finally, what policy measures are available for reducing the differentially high unemployment rates, and what are the costs involved in reducing these unemployment rates by various amounts?

We shall deal with the first several of these questions here and in Chapter 6. The last and most difficult question—what can be done and at what cost—will be considered (albeit far from comprehensively) in the final chapter.[1]

The Various Dimensions of the Labor Force

The labor force can be classified in various ways. The *Monthly Report on the Labor Force* breaks down the unemployment figures by age, sex, industry, occupation, color, marital status, household relationship, and duration of unemployment. In addition, special surveys provide us with information on unemployment by education level, and estimates are also made of unemployment on a regional basis. For our purposes, it will be enough to examine unemployment patterns by age, sex, color, occupation, industry, and education. These dimensions are sufficient to reveal the general character and magnitude of "structural unemployment" in the United States and the ways in which this type of unemployment has changed over the postwar years.

We are concerned with the differential incidence of unemployment involving each of the dimensions of the labor force that we have just enumerated and also with the way in which this incidence varies with the overall unemployment rate. We must therefore examine both the pattern of sectoral unemployment rates—by age, sex, color, and so on—and also the relative importance of the various sectors.

Measuring the Incidence of Unemployment

If unemployment rates for all sectors of the labor force were the same—and therefore equal to the overall unemployment rate—then each sector's fraction of total unemployment would be equal to its relative share of the labor force. This suggests one way of studying the pattern of unemployment: to compare each sector's share of total unemployment with its share of the labor force. It will help in the subsequent discussion if we introduce some simple algebraic notation:

Let U stand for the amount of unemployment and L for the absolute size of the labor force.

Let u stand for the unemployment *rate*, that is, U/L.

Let the subscript i stand for any particular sector of the labor force.

Then, the unemployment rate for any sector—say, male teenagers—would be

$$u_i = \frac{U_i}{L_i}$$

If we weight all the sectoral unemployment rates in any one dimension, such as occupation, and sum, we arrive at the overall unemployment rate.

$$\sum \left(u_i \cdot \frac{L_i}{L} \right) = \sum \left(\frac{U_i}{L_i} \cdot \frac{L_i}{L} \right) = \frac{U}{L} = u$$

Now any one sector's share of total unemployment can be expressed as:

$$\frac{u_i}{u} \cdot \frac{L_i}{L} = \frac{U_i}{L_i} \cdot \frac{L}{U} \cdot \frac{L_i}{L} = \frac{U_i}{U}$$

In other words, any particular sector's share of total unemployment can be resolved into two elements: (1) the ratio of the sector's unemployment rate to the overall rate u_i/u, multiplied by (2) its fraction of the labor force.

The suggestion that we compare each sector's fraction of total unemployment with its share of the labor force means considering the difference

$$\frac{U_i}{U} - \frac{L_i}{L}$$

which is the same as

$$\left(\frac{u_i}{u} \cdot \frac{L_i}{L} \right) - \frac{L_i}{L} = \frac{L_i}{L} \left(\frac{u_i}{u} - 1 \right)$$

If, along any dimension, we sum the absolute differences between each sector's relative contribution to total unemployment and its portion of the labor force, we have

$$\sum \left| \frac{U_i}{U} - \frac{L_i}{L} \right|$$

Let us use the symbol D_u to refer to this measure of the unequal incidence of unemployment.

If, for any particular classification of the labor force, unemployment rates for all sectors are equal, then U_i/U will be equal to L_i/L for every sector, and D_u will be equal to zero. If the sectoral unemployment rates are unequal, D_u will be positive. The wider the discrepancies between the various sectors' contributions to unemployment and to the labor force, the larger will be our measure.

The difference between U_i/U and L_i/L can be used not only when added for all groups in the labor force classified in a particular way; it also can be used to study the changing incidence of unemployment in any particular segment of the labor force. Thus, looking ahead to Table 6.1 (p. 119), we see that in 1959, U_i/U for male teen-agers was 11.8 per cent, whereas L_i/L was only 4.7 per cent. In 1965, the two percentages were, respectively, 15.8 and 5.5. Thus we have the following.

Year	U_i/U	L_i/L	Difference
1959	11.8	4.7	7.1
1965	15.8	5.5	10.3

The unemployment situation for male teen-agers had obviously worsened *relatively* between 1959 and 1965. Further examination of Table 6.1 indicates that this relative worsening came about *both* because the teen-age unemployment rate rose relative to the national rate *and* because male teen-agers became a larger part of the labor force. We observed that $U_i/U - L_i/L$ is the same as

$$\frac{L_i}{L}\left(\frac{u_i}{u} - 1\right)$$

Thus our measure for male teen-agers increased both because u_i/u rose from 2.51 to 2.85 and because L_i/L increased from 4.7 to 5.5 per cent of the total labor force.

If we examine the entire age-sex breakdown presented in Table 6.1, we observe that our total dispersion measure also increased between 1959 and 1965, from .321 to .497. This increase is largely (but not entirely) explained by the relatively worsened position of young people of both sexes in the age group 14–19.

Some Properties of Our Measure

Since we plan to make considerable use of the dispersion measure developed in the preceding section, it would be well to inspect it carefully at this point. The measure can be interpreted in either of two ways.

The common-sense interpretation. In the simplest terms, the measure shows by how much the relative contributions to total unemployment of the different sectors of the labor force differ from their relative proportions in the labor force. Some groups (youth, the unskilled, or nonwhites) will account for a much larger fraction of unemployment than of the labor force. For other groups, the reverse will be true. Both types of discrepancy increase the size of our dispersion measure.

A more technical interpretation. There is another way of interpreting our measure. It is a measure of dispersion of sectoral unemployment rates around the average unemployment rate for the entire labor force, with the difference between each sector's rate and the average being weighted by the sector's share of the labor force. This is nothing more than the familiar measure of dispersion called the *average deviation*. Furthermore, our measure is equivalent not to the absolute value of such an average deviation of sectoral unemployment rates but to the ratio of the average deviation to the average (or national) unemployment rate.

The algebraic demonstration of this is quite simple. We have already seen that, for any sector of the labor force, we can state:

$$\frac{U_i}{U} - \frac{L_i}{L} = \frac{L_i}{L}\left(\frac{u_i}{u} - 1\right)$$

$$= \frac{L_i}{L}\left(\frac{u_i - u}{u}\right)$$

Summing the last expression without regard to sign, we have:

$$\sum \left| \frac{L_i}{L}\left(\frac{u_i - u}{u}\right) \right| = \frac{1}{u} \sum \left| \frac{L_i}{L}\left(u_i - u\right) \right| = \frac{A_u}{u}$$

where A_u is the average deviation of sectoral unemployment rates. A_u measures the absolute dispersion of sectoral unemployment rates about the national unemployment rate, while D_u can be considered a measure of *relative* dispersion—relative to the overall unemployment rate.

When we put it in this form, we are able to learn much more about the characteristics of our dispersion index, D_u. This last formulation tells us that the index may change for any one of the following three reasons:

1. Individual sectors' unemployment rates (u_i) may disperse more widely around the national rate (u).

2. With a given dispersion of individual unemployment rates around the national rate, some sectors may come to represent a smaller or larger share of the labor force (L_i/L). If groups with relatively high unemployment rates increase their share of the labor force (for example, this happened in the last few years with teen-agers), the dispersion index will increase.

3. Both of the preceding characteristics of our index could be inferred from the simpler formulation in terms of the sum of the differences between proportions of total unemployment and contributions to the labor force. But our second formulation, in which our measure is seen to be an average deviation of sectoral unemployment rates divided by the national unemployment rate, reveals yet another characteristic of our index—a characteristic that may prove to be bothersome. Our measure may change merely because the overall unemployment rate rises or falls. Thus, even if all individual unemployment rates remain above or below the national rate by unchanging amounts, and even if all sectors maintain constant fractions of the labor force, our dispersion index will rise as the overall unemployment falls, and it will decline as the overall rate rises.

Thus we see that our measure D_u, which we shall refer to as the index of relative dispersion or, for short, the dispersion index,

$$\sum \left| \frac{U_i}{U} - \frac{L_i}{L} \right|$$

will vary inversely with the national unemployment rate even if there is no change in the absolute dispersion of unemployment rates. Or, to restate the situation, our index will change if u changes, even though there is no change in the average deviation of unemployment rates as measured by

$$A_u = \sum \left| \frac{L_i}{L} \left(u_i - u \right) \right|$$

Secular Changes in the Dispersion Index: A Preliminary View

Figures 5.1 through 5.4 present the annual values for our dispersion index during the postwar period for several dimensions of the labor force: age-sex, color, occupation, and industry. On each chart there is also plotted the average deviation of sectoral unemployment rates (just described), which in effect is our rela-

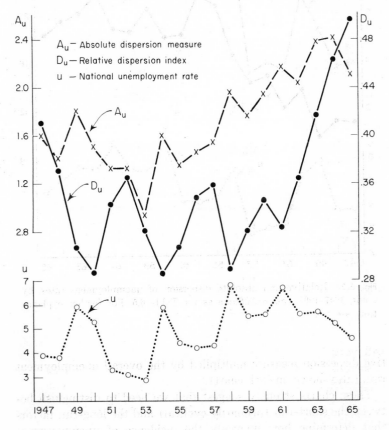

Fig. 5.1. Relative and absolute dispersion of unemployment rates, by age and sex, 1947–1965. (*Source:* Same as for Table 6.1. For further explanation, see text.)

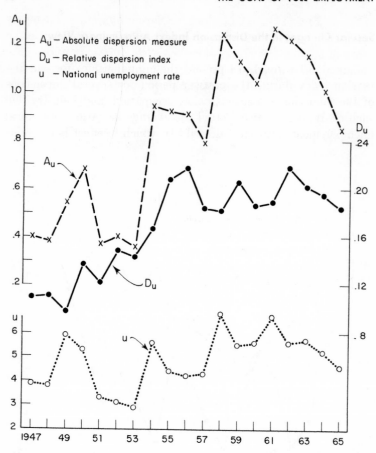

Fig. 5.2. Relative and absolute dispersion of unemployment rates, by color, 1947–1965. (*Source:* Same as for Table 6.5. For further explanation, see text.)

tive dispersion measure multiplied by the overall unemployment rate (also shown on each chart).

These charts strongly suggest that we need to distinguish between the short-run (primarily cyclical) and the long-run factors that determine how unevenly the incidence of unemployment is distributed. A cyclical and a longer-run movement can be detected in both dispersion measures.

In all four charts, the average deviation of sectoral unemployment rates (A_u) shows an upward trend—most marked in the case of age-sex and color—since the early 1950's. It is also clear, however, that a good deal of this upward trend is due simply to the rise in the overall unemployment rate. If we take our index

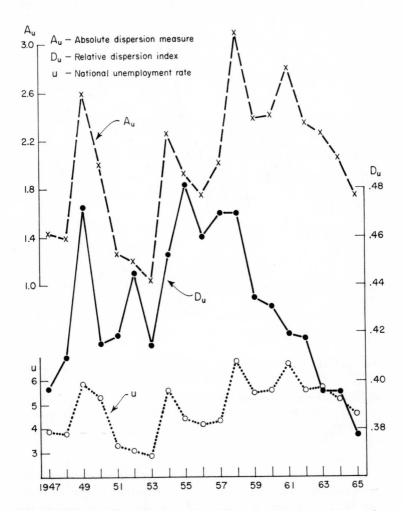

Fig. 5.3. Absolute and relative dispersion of unemployment rates, by occupation, excluding those without previous work experience, 1947–1965. (*Source:* Same as for Table 6.8. For further explanation, see text.)

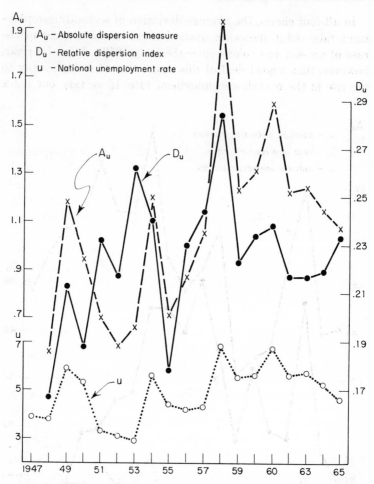

Fig. 5.4. Absolute and relative dispersion of unemployment rates, by industry, 1947–1965. (*Source:* Same as for Table 6.10. For further explanation, see text.)

of relative dispersion, D_u, which is equivalent to A_u divided by the unemployment rate, the upward trend since the early or mid-1950's is much less noticeable. In the case of age-sex the trend was downward until the early 1960's, after this the measure rose sharply. D_u declined markedly after 1955 for the occupational breakdown and was lower in 1965 than in any previous year in the postwar period. Our index for the industrial dimension of the labor force showed a rising trend until 1958 and then a declining trend.

Cyclical Patterns in Dispersion

Let us now inspect the cyclical behavior of our dispersion measures. This can best be done by considering Figs. 5.5 through 5.8, which show the behavior of our dispersion measures and the overall unemployment rate for each postwar business cycle. In general, we should expect the dispersion in sectoral unemployment rates along any dimension to widen as the national rate rises and to narrow as the national rate falls. In general, those groups which regularly experience high unemployment rates are likely to suffer more when employment conditions worsen than are those groups whose unemployment rates are regularly below the national average. On the whole, this turns out to be the case. The average deviation of unemployment rates generally tends to rise and fall over the cycle with the national unemployment rate.

The situation is somewhat different when we examine the cyclical behavior of our relative dispersion index. Here we must clearly distinguish between the behavior of the index for the age-sex and color breakdowns, on the one hand, and the cyclical pattern of the index in the case of the occupational and industrial classifications, on the other. The need for such a distinction is hardly surprising. By definition, movement of workers out of a particular age, color, or sex category—where physical characteristics are the basis of the classification—is impossible. (Over time, of course, a worker's age will change.) But movement is possible among industries and occupations. This basic difference in the degree of mobility possible should make a considerable difference in the way our dispersion measure behaves in the short run.

When we consider age-sex and color (Figs. 5.5–5.6), our relative dispersion index tends, on the whole, to move *inversely* with the national unemployment rate. When the latter falls during

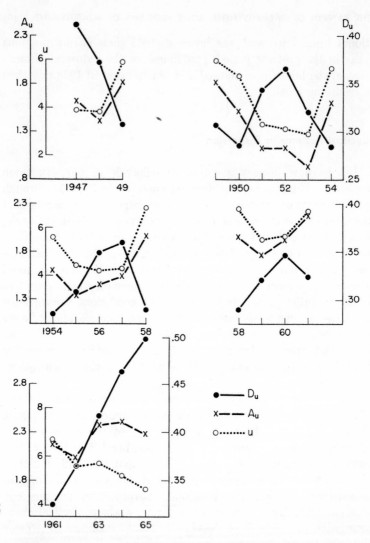

Fig. 5.5. Relative and absolute dispersion of unemployment rates by age and sex over successive postwar cycles, 1947–1965. (*Source:* Same data as in Fig. 5.1.)

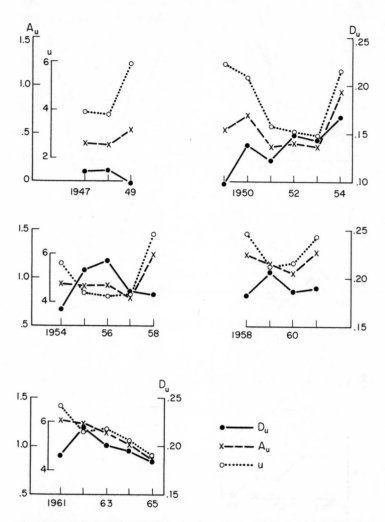

Fig. 5.6. Relative and absolute dispersion of unemployment rates by color over successive postwar cycles, 1947–1965. (*Source:* Same data as in Fig. 5.2.)

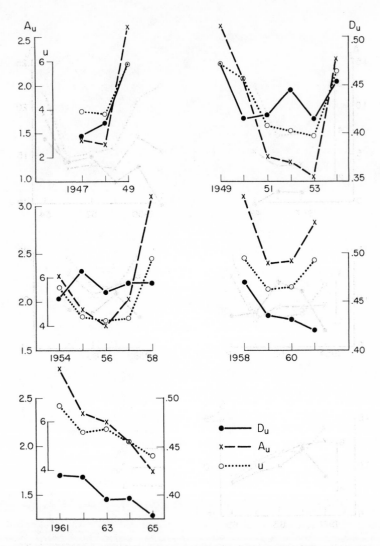

Fig. 5.7. Relative and absolute dispersion of unemployment rates by occupation over successive postwar cycles, 1947–1965. (Excludes those without previous work experience.) (*Source:* Same data as in Fig. 5.3.)

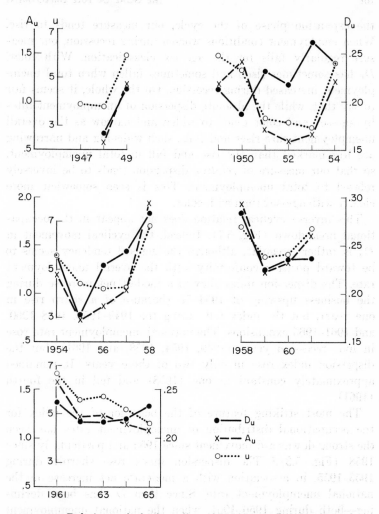

Fig. 5.8. Relative and absolute dispersion of unemployment rates by industry over successive postwar cycles, 1947–1965. (*Source:* Same data as in Fig. 5.4.)

the expansion phase of the cycle, our measure tends to rise. When employment conditions worsen during recession, our measure regularly falls for the age-sex classification. With color, D_u has sometimes risen and sometimes fallen when total unemployment increased during recession. On the whole, it seems fair to say that, while the absolute dispersion of unemployment rates by age-sex and color tends to widen and narrow as the overall unemployment rate rises and falls, such widening and narrowing are less marked than the rise and fall in total unemployment, so that our measure of *relative* dispersion tends to be inversely related to total unemployment. This is seen somewhat more clearly with age-sex than with color.

This inverse cyclical relation does not appear in the occupational breakdown (Fig. 5.7). Indeed, the cyclical movement in D_u is rather irregular, although the general tendency seems to be toward positive conformity with the overall unemployment rate. The dispersion index showed a modest net increase during the business upswing of 1954–57 (because of a sharp rise in one year), but the index fell during the 1949–1953, 1958–1960, and 1961–1965 expansions. The national unemployment rate rose in four recession years (1949, 1954, 1958, and 1961), but the dispersion index rose in only two of these years. It remained approximately constant in one (1958) and fell in the fourth (1961).

The most striking feature of the behavior of the index for the occupational distribution of unemployment rates has been the strong downward movement since 1955 and particularly since 1958 (Fig. 5.3).[2] The dispersion index rose sharply during 1953–1955, in association with a moderate net increase in the national unemployment rate. Since then D_u has been declining—both during 1956–1961, when the national unemployment rate rose, and during 1961–1965, when employment conditions generally were improving. This behavior of the dispersion index for occupational unemployment rates is the opposite of what is implied by the argument that "structural unemployment" in the United States worsened after the mid-1950's and that "structural factors" were largely responsible for the high overall level of unemployment in the late fifties and early sixties.

The pattern is different, however, if we include in our index those without previous work experience, who by definition have no occupational attachment. The proportion of the inexperienced group in total unemployment has been rising steadily since the early 1950's, and the increase in $(U_i/U - L_i/L)$ for this group since, say, 1956, has just about offset the decline in relative dispersion among occupational unemployment rates for experienced workers. The result is that D_u for the occupational breakdown of unemployment inclusive of those with no previous work experience has shown little net change in the last decade. We shall discuss this situation further in Chapter 6.

Let us now examine the cyclical behavior of the dispersion index for the industry breakdown of unemployment rates. The cyclical patterns delineated in Fig. 5.8 convey a rather mixed picture. During the cycles of 1954–1958 and 1958–1961, our relative dispersion measure seemed to reveal essentially the same cyclical behavior as the measure of absolute dispersion, and both moved in rough positive conformity with the overall unemployment rate. It would seem that at least since 1954, the two different measures of dispersion displayed in Fig. 5.8 have moved fairly closely together over the business cycle. The average deviation—measuring the absolute spread of industry unemployment rates—has shown a wider amplitude over the cycle than has the measure of total unemployment, with the result that our index of *relative* dispersion has also been positively correlated with the national unemployment rate.[3] This is just the opposite of what we found for the classifications by age and color.

D_u for the industry classification seems to have behaved differently during the 1949–1954 cycle than during the business cycles that followed. Here the relative and absolute measures did not tend to move together. During the expansion period (1949–1953) D_u rose irregularly and was considerably higher in 1953 than in 1949 or 1950. The absolute dispersion measure, in contrast, declined with the national unemployment rate. Furthermore, the relative dispersion index fell during the 1954 recession, whereas it rose during the 1949, 1958, and 1961 recessions.

There is one respect in which we can observe that D_u for the industry classification did behave similarly in all of the postwar cyclical expansions in economic activity. It *always* declined in the first year of recovery (in 1950, 1955, 1959, and 1962).[4] It then tended to rise during the rest of the upswing, although only during 1949–1953 did this increase carry the index significantly above its level at the preceding business trough.

Let us recapitulate briefly. Over the course of the cycle, our relative dispersion index tends to be inversely related to the overall unemployment rate in the case of age-sex and color; it is, on the whole, positively associated with the level of unemployment when we consider the dispersion of industry unemployment rates; and there seems also to be some modest but irregular association between the general level of unemployment and the relative dispersion of unemployment rates by occupation.

Thus the cyclical behavior of our dispersion index depends on the particular dimension of the labor force that we are considering. With age-sex and color, the tendency toward an inverse cyclical pattern reflects the fact that the absolute dispersion of unemployment rates does not decline, when employment expands, as rapidly as the unemployment rate falls. All age and color groups benefit when the national unemployment rate declines during business expansions, but the relatively high rates do not decline proportionately as much as does the overall rate. As a result, the groups with the highest unemployment rates make up an increasing proportion of a declining volume of total unemployment as employment conditions improve.

Figures 5.5 and 5.6 suggest one important qualification to these generalizations. In the late stages of cyclical expansion, the pressure of expanding demand may bring about an accelerated decline in relatively high unemployment rates (for example, of nonwhites and young workers), with the result that D_u may begin to decline. This happened with color toward the end of each of the postwar cyclical expansions from 1949 on, and the age-sex measure showed a similar decline in 1948 and 1953 (but not in 1957 or 1960). It is also worth noting that D_u for the color classification began to decline early during the long business expansion that began in 1961, and by 1965 was slightly below its level in 1961. In none of the previous postwar expansions did D_u by color show this sort of steady and prolonged decline.[5]

In contrast to the behavior of the unemployment differentials in the case of age, sex, and color, there does tend to be some irregular narrowing of relative unemployment-rate differentials on the upswing when we classify the labor force by industry. This narrowing comes particularly in the first years of the cyclical upswing and reflects the especially rapid decline in unemployment in durable-goods manufacturing, which accounted for from one-sixth to more than one-fifth of total unemployment in the various postwar recessions. On the whole, moreover, but in a somewhat irregular way, there is a relative narrowing of occupational unemployment rates as the total unemployment rate declines. This particularly reflects the relative cyclical improvement in the position of semiskilled operatives and unskilled laborers.

Structural Unemployment and the Dispersion Index

In Chapter 3, we attempted to describe briefly the nature and causes of structural unemployment. Let us see now to what extent our dispersion index, D_u, can help us to trace the course of structural unemployment in the United States in recent years.[6]

An increase in structural unemployment results from shifts in the *pattern* of demand for or supply of labor to which the economy finds it difficult to adjust because of some degree of labor immobility and wage inflexibility.[7] The notion of structural unemployment implies (1) a heterogeneous labor force, with unemployment rates higher for some sectors than for others when the economy is at aggregative full employment, (2) that these differentials in unemployment rates are greater than can be accounted for by sectoral differences in the rate of frictional unemployment, and (3) that labor immobility and wage inflexibility cause these unemployment differentials to persist over a series of years of aggregative full employment.[8]

To say that structural unemployment is increasing is to imply that, for one or more ways of classifying the labor force (for example, by age or occupation), there is a growing discrepancy between the pattern of labor supply and the pattern of labor demand. These supply and demand patterns should, of course, be compared for successive years of aggregative full employment—in order to eliminate purely cyclical effects.[9]

We suggest that our relative dispersion measure, D_u, taken

over a series of years approximating aggregative full employment, provides a reasonable test as to whether a significant
change in the amount of structural unemployment has occurred.
It might seem that an alternative measure, comparing the pattern
of *employment* with that of the labor force, might follow more
logically from our definition of structural unemployment. This
is a matter that is worth exploring briefly. Let E be the amount
of employment and e the rate of employment (that is, E/L).
Then we can write a measure of relative dispersion of employment rates, D_e, corresponding to D_u, as follows:

$$D_e = \sum \left| \frac{E_i}{E} - \frac{L_i}{L} \right|$$

It can be shown that these two measures of relative dispersion
are related in the following way:[10]

$$D_e = \left(\frac{u}{1-u} \right) D_u$$

Further, we already know that

$$D_u = \frac{\sum \left| (u_i - u) \dfrac{L_i}{L} \right|}{u} = \frac{A_u}{u}$$

which is the average deviation (A_u) divided by the unemployment rate. By substituting into the previous equation, we have

$$D_e = \left(\frac{u}{1-u} \right) \frac{A_u}{u} = \frac{A_u}{1-u}$$

Thus the measure of *relative* dispersion of *employment* rates
turns out to be equal to the measure of *absolute* dispersion of
unemployment rates divided by the overall rate of employment
(or one minus the overall unemployment rate). But this denominator stays within a relatively narrow range (in the United
States, this is between, say, .93 and .97). Both the trend (if any)
and year-to-year changes in D_e will correspond to the behavior
of A_u, and we have already seen that the latter measure of absolute dispersion is heavily influenced by the level of the overall
rate of unemployment. This is illustrated in Figs. 5.9 and 5.10,
which show the three measures, D_e, D_u, and A_u for two classifi-

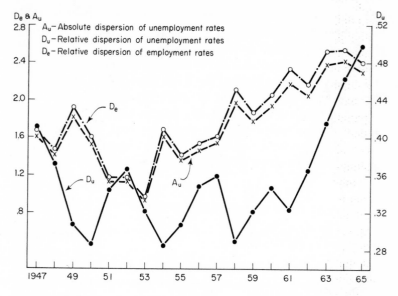

Fig. 5.9. Relative and absolute dispersion of unemployment rates and relative dispersion of employment rates, by age and sex, 1947–1965. (*Source:* Same as for Table 6.1. For further explanation, see text.)

cations of the labor force. Hence whatever merits D_u has over A_u in tracing changes in the pattern of unemployment, including those changes we call structural, it will also have, to nearly the same degree, with respect to D_e.

Our choice of D_u can be further rationalized as follows. At aggregative full employment, the excess of the unemployment rate for any group over the frictional minimum is a measure of the imbalance between demand and supply for that particular kind of labor, given existing wage differentials. The difference between the group's unemployment rate and the national rate will reflect both this structural imbalance and the amount by which the rate of frictional unemployment for that group varies from the average rate of frictional unemployment for the labor force as a whole. If there is no change in frictional unemployment, but increasing imbalance between supply of and demand for the labor of this group causes its unemployment rate to rise, even though aggregative full employment is maintained, we can fairly say that the increased deviation of this group's

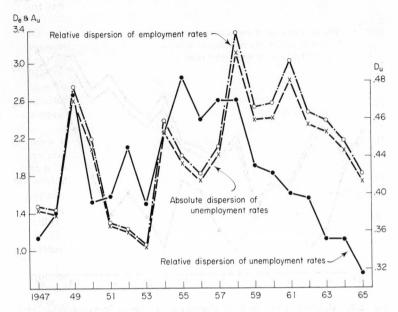

Fig. 5.10. Relative and absolute dispersion of unemployment rates and relative dispersion of employment rates, by occupation, 1947–1965. (*Source:* Same as for Table 6.8. For further explanation, see text. Data are for experienced workers only.)

unemployment rate from the national rate (weighted by its share of the labor force) is a measure of the extent to which structural unemployment in this sector has worsened. It would seem appropriate to measure, as well, this worsening relative to the overall unemployment rate. If a group's unemployment rate is two percentage points higher than the national rate, this is relatively a more serious matter when the national rate is only 2 per cent than when it is 4 per cent.

This discussion also suggests several cautions about the use of D_u either as a measure of the amount of structural unemployment at a given time or of the change in structural unemployment over a period of time. First, clearly, if the measure is to reveal something about changes in structural unemployment, we should compare only years in which we think there was a reasonably close approximation to aggregative full employment.[11] Thus the usefulness of the measure for this purpose is limited for studying those periods characterized by a significant deficiency of aggregate demand, for example, during 1958–1964 in the United States. Fortunately, in the last year of the period we plan to examine, 1965, the American economy was again approaching full employment.[12] Second, it might be mentioned that, even at aggregative full employment. D_u measures differences in frictional as well as structural unemployment (as we have defined it). Third, even if these first two cautions are observed, it can be argued that there is some slight inherent bias in the use of D_u to measure changes in structural unemployment, although the bias is not likely to be serious in most cases.

This bias results from the fact that a change in structural unemployment affects the level of unemployment corresponding to aggregative full employment. Use of D_u to measure the change in structural unemployment between two periods means that in effect we compute ΔD_u, where

$$\Delta D_u = \frac{1}{u_{t+1}} \sum \left| \frac{L_i}{L} (u_i - u) \right|_{t+1} - \frac{1}{u_t} \sum \left| \frac{L_i}{L} (u_i - u) \right|_t$$

If structural unemployment increases, u_{t+1} will presumably be greater than u_t, and this will reduce the size of ΔD_u. Similarly, if structural unemployment declines, u_{t+1} will be less than u_t and this will increase the size of ΔD_t for a given change in the weighted dispersion of unemployment rates. One possible solution would be to divide the absolute dispersion measure in each of the two periods by the same unemployment rate, say, that prevailing in the first of the two periods.

One more caution about the use of our dispersion index must be mentioned. Our entire discussion has assumed that a worsening of structural unemployment occurs through a rise in sectoral unemployment rates that are already high relative to the national rate. However, suppose that there is an increase in a relatively low unemployment rate, all other sectoral unemployment rates remaining the same. The result will be to reduce A_u and D_u (and also to raise somewhat the value of u corresponding to full employment). In this case, any measure of dispersion will fail to reveal the increase in structural unemployment.[13] As a practical matter, however, the debate about structural unemployment in the United States has been associated with the presumed worsening of the position of groups whose unemployment rates have been relatively high.

We should also mention that throughout this discussion we have assumed that we need only be concerned with those who are officially recorded as being in the labor force. If recorded unemployment is considerably above the frictional minimum, however, there may be some quantity of what (in Chapter 3) we have termed disguised unemployment; that is, some persons may want to work but may fail to look for work because no jobs are available. Since such disguised unemployment varies with recorded unemployment among different groups, our dispersion index based on recorded unemployment will tend to understate the extent of the imbalance between the patterns of demand and supply in the labor market, and the higher the overall unemployment rate, the greater the understatement.[14] Similar considerations apply with respect to involuntary part-time work. We shall give some attention to this range of problems in Chapter 6.

In the preceding paragraphs, we have tried to protect the reader by mentioning all the limitations of our dispersion measure that have occurred to us. Despite these limitations, the measure can, if carefully used, reveal something about changes in structural unemployment in the United States during the years since World War II. And, as we have seen, the measure has already proved useful in tracing changes in the cyclical pattern of unemployment.

Keeping these various cautions in mind, let us proceed now to a more detailed consideration of the changing pattern of unemployment in the United States in the postwar years. Our chief tools for this purpose will be those which we have developed in this chapter.

NOTES

1. This chapter and Chapter 6 represent an elaboration and updating of my paper, "Has Structural Unemployment Worsened?" *Industrial Relations,* **III** (May 1964), 53–77. For an econometric approach to some of the questions discussed in this and the following chapter, see L. C. Thurow,

"The Changing Structure of Unemployment: An Econometric Study," *Review of Economics and Statistics,* **XLVII** (May 1965), 137–149.

2. This is true for *experienced* workers—excluding those with no previous work experience. The fraction of the latter in total unemployment has increased significantly since the early 1950's.

3. During 1963–1965, however, D_u rose while both A_u and the national unemployment rate fell.

4. D_u for the occupational classification fell in the first year of the 1949–1953, 1958–1960, and 1961–1965 upswings but not in the first year of the 1954–1957 expansion.

5. After this was written, the Bureau of Labor Statistics reported a considerable rise in u_i/u and U_i/U for nonwhites during the spring and summer of 1966. On a seasonally adjusted basis $(U_i/U - L_i/L)$ was higher in the third quarter of 1966 than it had been in any calendar year during the preceding decade. For 1966 as a whole, u_i/u for nonwhites turned out to be higher than it had been since 1962. The same was true of D_u by color.

6. Some questions about the use of our dispersion measure for this purpose have been raised by R. G. Lipsey. See his paper, "Structural and Deficient Demand Unemployment Reconsidered," in A. M. Ross (ed.), *Employment Policy and the Labor Market* (Berkeley: University of California Press, 1965), pp. 240–241. See also Vladimir Stoikov, "Increasing Structural Unemployment Reexamined," *Industrial and Labor Relations Review,* **XIX** (April 1966), 368–376. These criticisms have been kept in mind in the discussion which follows here and in Chapter 6.

7. George Hildebrand, among others, has emphasized the role of wages in creating structural unemployment, arguing that the labor market has "overvalued unskilled and inexperienced workers relative to the more skilled groups." See his paper in Jack Stieber (ed.), *Employment Problems of Automation and Advanced Technology: An International Perspective* (London: Macmillan, 1966), pp. 105–127. (The quotation is from p. 126.) See also G. H. Hildebrand and G. E. Delehanty, "Wage Levels and Differentials," in R. A. Gordon and M. S. Gordon (ed.), *Prosperity and Unemployment* (New York: Wiley, 1966), pp. 265–301. The latter paper contains a useful bibliography.

8. For a similar characterization of the nature of structural unemployment, see Robert M. Solow, *The Nature and Sources of Unemployment in the United States* (Stockholm: Almquist and Wiksell, 1964), pp. 20–21. In an as yet unpublished study for the Brookings Institution, Barbara Bergmann and David Kaun have sought to estimate the amount of structural unemployment in the United States in 1964 and the amount by which it had changed during the preceding decade. For a useful survey and critique of various earlier attempts to measure the postwar change in structural unemployment in the United States, see the paper by R. G. Lipsey previously cited, as well as the more recent article by V. Stoikov, also previously cited. In an as yet unpublished paper, W. H. Gruber and M. Cohen explore a large number of possible sources of

bias in the efforts that have been made to determine whether structural unemployment has increased in the postwar period.

9. An increase in structural unemployment will, of course, increase the amount of unemployment that corresponds to aggregative full employment.

10. We know that

$$D_u = \frac{1}{u} \sum \left| \frac{L_i}{L} (u_i - u) \right|$$

Similarly,

$$D_e = \frac{1}{e} \sum \left| \frac{L_i}{L} (e_i - e) \right|$$

$$= \frac{1}{1 - u} \sum \left| \frac{L_i}{L} (1 - u_i - 1 + u) \right|$$

$$= \frac{1}{1 - u} \sum \left| \frac{L_i}{L} (u - u_i) \right|$$

Thus

$$\frac{D_e}{D_u} = \frac{u}{1 - u} \quad \text{and} \quad D_e = \frac{u}{1 - u} D_u$$

11. This condition, in effect, is the same which Lipsey has used to argue that the characteristics of the unemployed tell us nothing about structural unemployment if some deficiency of aggregate demand exists. See Lipsey, *op. cit.*, pp. 241, 246–252.

12. See the further discussion of this point in the introductory section of Chapter 6.

13. This point is made in Lipsey, *op. cit.*, p. 231.

14. Various attempts have been made (for example, by Bowen and Finegan, Cain, Cooper and Johnston, Dernberg and Strand, and Tella) to measure the amount of disguised unemployment in recent years by studying the relation between labor force participation rates for various groups, on the one hand, and the overall unemployment rate and other variables, on the other. For a useful evaluation of these studies, see the excellent paper by Jacob Mincer, "Labor-Force Participation and Unemployment: A Review of Recent Evidence," in Gordon and Gordon (eds.), *op. cit.*, pp. 73–112. See also the recent paper by Dernburg and Strand, "Hidden Unemployment, 1953–62: A Quantitative Analysis by Age and Sex," *American Economic Review*, LVI (March 1966), 71–95. For an interesting attempt to adjust our measure for disguised unemployment, see R. J. Flanagan, "Disguised Unemployment and the Structural Hypothesis," *Industrial Relations*, V (October 1965), 23–36.

CHAPTER 6

Changing Patterns of Unemployment
in the United States

We now proceed to further consideration of the changing pattern of unemployment in the United States since World War II, keeping in mind the limitations of the measures that we have presented. For each of the chief classifications of the labor force, we shall examine the relation of U_i to L_i, confining our attention to the years in which unemployment reached its cyclical low. To do this we shall not only use our dispersion index but also consider the individual sectors along each of the main dimensions of the labor force.

Since there were no years between 1958 and 1965 during which the United States enjoyed a condition of aggregative full employment (on an annual basis), use of our relative dispersion index cannot give clear-cut answers to the questions of whether structural unemployment has been increasing and in what ways. But careful study of the behavior of the index over a succession of business cycles, particularly when supplemented by a review of the behavior of $(U_i/U - L_i/L)$ for individual sectors of the labor force, should throw some light on underlying structural trends. And by 1965, the overall unemployment rate had fallen to an annual average of 4.6 per cent (it was as low as 4 per cent by the end of the year). Given the changed age-sex composition of the labor force since the mid-1950's, an unemployment rate of 4 per cent in 1956 corresponded to a rate of about 4.2 per cent in 1965.[1] Thus the 1965 rate of 4.6 per cent probably did not represent a much greater departure from aggregative full employment than the 4.2 per cent rate in 1956 (assuming no change in the welfare function relating unemployment to the other target variables).

Unemployment by Age and Sex

Let us consider first the age-sex breakdown in Table 6.1. Here, for each of the postwar years in which unemployment reached a cyclical low, we present three columns corresponding to the three elements in our basic identity. Column A gives the ratio of the unemployment rate for each age-sex group to the national rate (that is, u_i/u); column B tells us what percentage of the civilian labor force was in each group (L_i/L); and column C, which can be viewed as the product of the first two columns, presents a percentage distribution of total unemployment by age and sex (U_i/U). In addition to 1948, 1953, 1956, and 1959—the years of lowest unemployment in each of the complete business cycles of the postwar period—we include 1965, the most recent year for which annual data were available at the time this was written.

If we look first at our index of relative dispersion, D_u (last line of the table), we see that the incidence of unemployment became slightly less uneven in the decade up to 1959, despite the upward drift in the national unemployment rate from 3.8 per cent in 1948 and 2.9 per cent in 1953 to 4.2 per cent in 1956 and 5.5 per cent in 1959. The reversal in trend after 1959 is dramatic. There was a gratifying decline in the overall unemployment rate between 1959 and 1965, but D_u rose by more than 50 per cent. If we refer to Fig. 5.1, which charts D_u on an annual basis, we see that this "structural" worsening seems to have begun about 1961. The national unemployment rate was about the same in 1961 as in 1958, but our dispersion measure was considerably higher. We observed in Chapter 5 that D_u for the age-sex dimension typically rises as employment conditions improve on the upswing of the cycle. After 1961, however, the rise in D_u considerably exceeded that in any of the other postwar upswings in employment (and also started from a higher level than in any other postwar recession). By 1965, with an unemployment rate

TABLE 6.1. Age-Sex Classification of the Civilian Labor Force and the Unemployed, Selected Years, 1948–1965[a]

Age and Sex	1948[c]			1953			1956			1959			1965		
	A	B	C	A	B	C	A	B	C	A	B	C	A	B	C
Males															
14–19	2.37	5.2	12.3	2.52	4.5	11.2	2.43	4.6	11.2	2.51	4.7	11.8	2.85	5.5	15.8
20–24	1.82	7.6	13.9	1.72	4.8	8.1	1.64	5.2	8.5	1.58	5.7	9.0	1.37	6.5	9.0
25–44	0.68	32.4	22.5	0.72	33.2	23.7	0.69	31.6	22.2	0.76	30.6	23.3	0.59	27.8	16.7
45–64	0.74	22.3	16.3	0.86	22.8	19.4	0.76	22.5	17.2	0.78	22.7	17.8	0.61	22.2	13.7
65 and over	0.89	3.9	3.5	0.83	4.0	3.2	0.83	3.9	3.2	0.87	3.3	2.9	0.76	2.8	2.2
Total	0.95	71.4	68.4	0.97	69.3	65.7	0.90	67.8	62.3	0.96	67.1	64.9	0.87	64.8	57.3
Females															
14–19	2.16	3.4	7.3	2.34	3.0	7.1	2.57	3.2	8.4	2.24	3.2	7.2	3.11	3.9	12.2
20–24	1.29	4.4	5.7	1.48	3.8	5.6	1.50	3.6	5.5	1.47	3.6	5.2	1.59	4.4	7.1
25–44	0.95	12.6	12.1	1.00	13.8	13.9	1.02	13.8	14.3	1.00	13.4	14.3	1.09	13.3	14.4
45–64	0.82	7.4	6.0	0.83	9.0	7.2	0.86	10.4	9.0	0.76	11.5	8.7	0.68	12.3	8.2
65 and over	0.61	0.8	0.5	0.48	1.1	0.5	0.55	1.2	0.7	0.51	1.2	0.6	0.61	1.3	0.8
Total	1.11	28.6	31.6	1.14	30.7	34.3	1.17	32.2	37.8	1.07	32.9	35.1	1.20	35.2	42.7
National unemployment rate		3.8			2.9			4.2			5.5			4.6	
Relative dispersion index[b]		0.371			0.321			0.348			0.321			0.497	

Source: Manpower Report of the President, March 1966, Statistical Appendix.

[a]The national and age-sex unemployment rates for 1956 and earlier years have been adjusted to reflect changes in definitions adopted subsequently. All data in the table reflect these revisions.

[b]This measure is explained in detail in Chapter 5. It is the sum of the absolute differences between the fraction of total unemployment and the fraction of the total civilian labor force accounted for by each group.

[c]Column headings:

A. Ratio of group's unemployment rate to national unemployment rate.

B. Percentage of civilian labor force in each group.

C. Percentage of total unemployment in each group.

119

TABLE 6.2. Differences between Female Shares of Total Unemployment and of the
Civilian Labor Force, by Age Groups, Selected Years, 1948-1965

Age Group	$U_i/U - L_i/L$ (in per cent)				
	1948	1953	1956	1959	1965
14-19	3.9	4.1	5.2	4.0	8.3
20-24	1.3	1.8	1.9	1.6	2.7
25-44	-0.5	0.1	0.5	-0.1	1.1
45-64	-1.4	-1.8	-1.4	-2.8	-4.1
65 and over	-0.3	-0.6	-0.5	-0.6	-0.5
Total	3.0	3.6	5.6	2.2	7.5

Source: Derived from Table 6.1.

of 4.6 per cent, D_u was at its highest value in the entire postwar
period and more than 40 per cent higher than it was in 1956,
when the national unemployment rate was 4.2 per cent.[2]

As is well known, this structural worsening along the age-sex
dimension is primarily a reflection of the deteriorating position
of young people in the job market. This is particularly true
of teen-agers. However, according to our measure, there has also
been some relative worsening in the position of women in the
labor market.

Dealing with this latter trend first, we present in Table 6.2 the
figures for $(U_i/U - L_i/L)$ for each of the female age groups
that can be derived from Table 6.1. These values suggest some
relative worsening of the employment situation for women between 1948 and 1956, with a rise in $(U_i/U - L_i/L)$ for all of
the age groups under 45. During the general increase in unemployment between 1956 and 1959 (with the national rate rising
from 4.2 to 5.5 per cent), the *relative* position of women improved—in part because women are more likely than men to
withdraw from or not enter the labor force if jobs are not available and in part because between 1956 and 1959 female employ-

ment rose considerably faster than male.[3] (The occupations and industries in which employment rose least during 1956–1959 were generally those in which males constitute a particularly large fraction of all workers.)[4]

Tables 6.1 and 6.2 both point to a significant relative deterioration in the employment situation of women between 1959 and 1965. For all age groups, the absolute sum of $(U_i/U - L_i/L)$ rose from 2.2 to 7.5 (per cent). A large part of this deterioration was concentrated in the 14–19 age group, but there was some moderate worsening in the 20–24 and 25–44 age groups also. *Relative* unemployment rates (u_i/u) rose for all female age groups under 45, but most markedly so for teen-agers. In contrast, the relative position of women aged 45–64 continued the improvement which had been sustained, with a mild interruption during the mid-fifties, since the end of the war. While their portion of the labor force continued to increase, their unemployment rate fell faster than the national rate. In 1965, their contribution to unemployment was more than 4 percentage points less than their fraction of the labor force, the highest difference that had been recorded in the postwar period.

We now inspect the changing incidence of unemployment by age. Table 6.1 brings out the relatively favorable position occupied by men in the prime working-age groups, 25–44 and 45–64 years. Their unemployment rates are below the national average, and their proportion of unemployment is considerably less than their fraction of the labor force. It is worth noting that the proportion of the labor force made up of men 25–44 years of age has declined significantly in the last dozen years (column B for the various years in Table 6.1). We should also point out the fact that the position of men 45–64 years of age has not deteriorated; at least, this deterioration is not evident with the measures that we are using. For this group, u_i/u was 0.61 in 1965, the lowest ratio appearing for any of the years shown in Table 6.1; and this sector's share of total unemployment was also lowest in 1965. Our measure $(U_i/U - L_i/L)$ yields a negative figure of —8.5 per cent in 1965, compared to a range of —3.4 to —6.0 for the earlier years in Table 6.1. In short, relative to their share of the labor force, men in this more mature age group suffered less unemployment in 1965 than they did during the peak years 1948, 1953, and 1956, when the overall unemployment rate was lower than it was in 1965.[5]

We now proceed to the youth unemployment problem and consider first the case of young adults in the 20–24 age group. Contrary to general impressions, the *relative* unemployment rate for young men aged 20 to 24 has fallen significantly over the postwar period and was lower in 1965 than in the 1950's.[6] This group's share of the labor force reached a low in 1954 (4.7 per cent) and has since risen to 6.5 per cent in 1965. Its proportion of unemployment has not risen correspondingly, with the result that in 1965 this group's share of unemployment was only 2.5 percentage points greater than its share of the labor force (Table 6.3). Except for the year 1951, this was the smallest difference

TABLE 6.3.　Proportions of Total Unemployment and Civilian Labor Force Accounted for by 14-19 and 20-24 Age Groups, by Sex, 1948-1965[a] (per cent)

Sex	Age Group					
	14–19			20–24		
	U_i/U	L_i/L	Difference	U_i/U	L_i/L	Difference
Males						
1948	12.3	5.2	7.1	13.9	7.6	6.3
1953	11.2	4.5	6.7	8.1	4.8	3.3
1956	11.2	4.6	6.6	8.5	5.2	3.3
1959	11.8	4.7	7.1	9.0	5.7	3.3
1961	11.3	4.9	6.4	9.5	5.9	3.6
1962	11.8	4.9	6.9	9.5	6.0	3.5
1963	13.6	5.0	8.6	9.5	6.2	3.3
1964	14.3	5.1	9.2	9.9	6.4	3.5
1965	15.8	5.5	10.3	9.0	6.5	2.5
Females						
1948	7.3	3.4	3.9	5.7	4.4	1.3
1953	7.1	3.0	4.1	5.6	3.8	1.8
1956	8.4	3.2	5.2	5.5	3.6	1.9
1959	7.2	3.2	4.0	5.2	3.6	1.6
1961	7.9	3.6	4.3	5.5	3.8	1.7
1962	8.6	3.6	5.0	6.4	3.9	2.5
1963	9.9	3.6	6.3	6.3	4.1	2.2
1964	10.6	3.7	6.9	7.1	4.3	2.8
1965	12.2	3.9	8.3	7.1	4.4	2.7

Source:　Manpower Reports of the President, Statistical Appendix.

[a]U_i/U is the proportion of total unemployment in each group; L_i/L is the proportion of the labor force in each group. These figures are expressed as percentages.

in the entire postwar period, and, as Table 6.3 indicates, lower than in the "full employment" years 1948, 1953, or 1956. The relative improvement for this group was particularly marked between 1964 and 1965.

The situation for young women (20 to 24 years old) is different. Here there has been some relative deterioration over the postwar years. This group's relative unemployment rate was somewhat higher in the 1950's than it had been in the early postwar years, and it was higher in 1965 than in the years of lowest unemployment in the fifties. This sector's share of the labor force began to rise after 1959 (Table 6.3); its proportion of unemployment rose even more. Contrary to the experience of males in the same age group, little improvement occurred between 1964 and 1965. Our measure $(U_i/U - L_i/L)$ was higher for females 20–24 years of age in 1964 and 1965 than it had been in any previous year in the postwar period.

Now we study the teen-agers. Table 6.1 informs us immediately that unemployment rates for youth under the age of 20 have been and are tragically high—well over twice the national average. We have here a "structural" problem of the first importance. This we all know.

However, Tables 6.1 and 6.3 indicate much more than this. First, there was little worsening of the teen-age unemployment problem (particularly in the case of boys) from the end of World War II to the beginning of the 1960's—a finding which is in contrast to general impressions.[7] Second, a significant deterioration in the teen-agers' relative position in the labor market suddenly began to appear in the early 1960's. This relative worsening can be dated from the years 1962–1963.[8]

Relative unemployment rates rose significantly for both girls and boys in 1963, and so did their percentages of total unemployment (Table 6.3). Relative deterioration continued during 1964 and 1965. For boys $(U_i/U - L_i/L)$ (expressed as a difference in percentages) rose from 6.9 in 1962 and 8.6 in 1963 to 9.2 in 1964 and 10.3 in 1965. These last two figures were the highest for this measure during the postwar period. Relatively, the deterioration was even more serious for girls; $(U_i/U - L_i/L)$ more than doubled for the female 14–19 age group between 1959 and 1965, with most of the increase coming after 1962. In terms

of the excess of their share of unemployment over their share
of the labor force, the relative position of girls had worsened
considerably more than that of boys since the mid-1950's (Table
6.3).[9]

Youth unemployment will continue to be a serious problem
during the rest of the 1960's. The teen-age component of the
labor force will continue to expand more rapidly than the labor
force as a whole. By 1970, according to official projections, the
14–19 age group will account for about 10 per cent of the total
labor force, compared to 9.6 per cent in 1965.[10] Obviously, a
manpower program aimed at achieving what we have called
"structural full employment" must be concerned with bringing
about a substantial reduction in the high unemployment rates
for this growing segment of the labor force.

The reader should be warned that our discussion has been
highly aggregative in the sense that it has combined the 14–17
age group, most of whom are in school, and those 18 and 19,
the majority of whom are not in school. And we have not sepa-
rated those in school, who seek chiefly part-time work, from

TABLE 6.4.   Distribution of Teen-Age Unemployment by Age and Sex, 1956-1965
(per cent)

Age Group	1956	1959	1963	1964	1965
Males					
14–15	8.3	7.3	6.6	6.9	6.8
16–17	24.3	26.3	25.3	26.7	25.6
18–19	24.5	28.5	25.7	23.9	24.0
Total	57.2	62.0	57.8	57.5	56.5
Females					
14–15	5.1	2.8	3.2	2.5	2.5
16–17	17.6	15.1	17.6	18.6	17.0
18–19	20.3	20.1	21.6	21.5	23.9
Total	42.8	38.0	42.2	42.5	43.5

Source: Manpower Report of the President, March 1966, Statistical Appendix.

those not in school, the great majority of whom want full-time jobs.

Table 6.4 throws some light on this range of questions. We may dismiss the 14 and 15-year-olds looking for part-time work. They made up less than 10 per cent of recorded teen-age unemployment in 1965, and the percentage has been declining. The proportion of teen-age unemployment accounted for by boys in the 16–17 age group in 1965 was a bit higher than it was in 1956 but slightly lower than in 1959. Girls in this age group do not seem to have contributed more to teen-age unemployment in 1965 than 1956. But girls 18 and 19, most of them out of school, did account for a significantly larger fraction of teen-age unemployment in 1965 than in 1956. This was not the situation for boys, in this age group. In 1965, boys and girls aged 18–19 accounted, respectively, for about 24 per cent of total teen-age unemployment. In the late 1950's boys of this age had contributed considerably more to teen-age unemployment than girls.

The percentage of unemployed teen-agers not in school has been declining over the postwar period, as is suggested by the following table.

PERCENTAGE OF UNEMPLOYED IN 16–17 AND 18–19 AGE GROUPS[a]
NOT IN SCHOOL, 1953–1964[a]

	Age Group	
Year	16–17	18–19
1953	68.3	89.1
1956	47.8	82.5
1959	49.8	86.9
1963	39.8	82.3
1964	31.7	83.3

[a] Figures are for October of each year. Computed from data in *Manpower Report of the President*, March 1966, Statistical Appendix. The data from 1959 on are not strictly comparable with those for earlier years.

The proportions, however, are still substantial. More than 80 per cent of unemployed 18- and 19-year-olds at the end of 1964 were not in school; this was also true of nearly one-third of those in the 16–17 age bracket. For the latter group the figure was about 50 per cent as recently as 1959.[11] Although, as we have noted, the percentage of the teen-age unemployed not in school has been declining, teen-age unemployment still represents predominantly a search for full-time jobs by young people no longer in school.[12] A policy of "structural" as well as "aggregative" full employment must seek to bring about a significant decline in the very high unemployment rate among teen-agers (in as well as out of school). In 1965 this rate was nearly three times that for the labor force as a whole.

Unemployment by Color

The civil rights movement of the last few years has dramatized the distressing plight of Negroes and other nonwhites in the labor market. How serious is the structural disadvantage suffered by nonwhites in finding jobs, and has this handicap grown more or less severe over the years since World War II? Table 6.5 provides some partial answers to these questions.[13]

Our relative dispersion index for the color-sex classification of the labor force doubled between 1948 and 1956, but then the rise stopped. D_u was little higher in 1965 than in 1956. (Indeed, the measure was lower in each of the years 1957–64 than in 1956.[14]) But here we need to distinguish the separate effects of color and sex. The small rise in our dispersion index between 1956 and 1965 is due entirely to the worsened position of women in the labor market. If we observe just the nonwhites, of both sexes, we see that (1) the relative unemployment rate (u_i/u) for nonwhite males declined significantly after 1959, and in 1965 was about the same as it had been in 1953; (2) the relative unemployment rate for nonwhite females rose between 1959 and 1965 (and somewhat more than it did for white females), but this rise did not fully offset the decline between 1956 and 1959; and (3) the nonwhite proportion of total unemployment was slightly less in 1965 than in 1956 or 1959, the

TABLE 6.5.   Color-Sex Classification of the Civilian Labor Force and the Unemployed, Selected Years, 1948–1965

Color and Sex	1948[b] A	1953[b] A	1956[c] A	1956[c] B	1956[c] C	1959 A	1959 B	1959 C	1965 A	1965 B	1965 C
Total White	0.95	0.93	0.88	89.3	78.5	0.89	89.1	78.8	0.89	88.9	79.7
Male	0.89	0.90	0.81	61.2	49.7	0.84	60.5	51.0	0.78	58.3	46.4
Female	1.03	1.07	1.02	28.1	28.8	0.96	28.6	27.8	1.09	30.6	33.3
Total Nonwhite	1.55	1.55	2.00	10.7	21.6	1.95	10.9	21.2	1.80	11.1	20.3
Male	1.50	1.66	1.90	6.6	12.6	2.09	6.6	13.8	1.65	6.5	10.9
Female	1.61	1.41	2.14	4.2	9.0	1.73	4.3	7.4	2.02	4.6	9.4
National unemployment rate	3.8	2.9		4.2			5.5			4.6	
Relative dispersion index[a]	0.111	0.152			0.230			0.206			0.238

Source: Manpower Report of the President, March 1966, Statistical Appendix.

[a]This measure is explained in detail in Chapter 5.   It is the sum of the absolute differences between the fraction of total unemployment and the fraction of the total civilian labor force accounted for by each group.

[b]Figures for the distribution of the labor force and of unemployment by color and sex have not been published for these years.   The dispersion index for 1948 and 1953 is based on unpublished data kindly made available by the Bureau of Labor Statistics.

[c]Column headings:

A.   Ratio of group's unemployment rate to national unemployment rate.
B.   Percentage of civilian labor force in each group.
C.   Percentage of total unemployment in each group.

TABLE 6.6.   Difference Between Nonwhite Fractions of Total Unemployment and of the Labor Force, by Sex, 1956-1965 (per cent)

Year	Male	Female	Total Nonwhite
1956	6.0	4.8	10.9
1959	7.2	3.1	10.3
1961	6.1	3.4	9.5
1962	6.4	4.5	10.8
1963	5.6	4.5	10.1
1964	4.8	4.9	9.7
1965	4.4	4.8	9.2

Source: Derived from the same source as the figures in Table 6.5.   The figures in each column express in percentage terms our measure $(\underline{U_i}/\underline{U} - \underline{L_i}/\underline{L})$.

fraction for males falling more than the fraction for females rose. On the whole, it is fair to state that the position of nonwhites in the labor market deteriorated markedly up to 1956 but, taking the two sexes together, there has been some slight improvement in the last few years.[15] These tendencies are further delineated by the figures for $(U_i/U - L_i/L)$ in Table 6.6.

The improvement in the position of nonwhite males since 1959 is clearly revealed in Table 6.6. The position of nonwhite females improved between 1956 and 1959, deteriorated between 1959 and 1964, and improved very slightly in 1965. For both sexes combined, there is moderate improvement since 1962, with the 1965 figure for $(U_i/U - L_i/L)$ being significantly lower than that in 1956, when the national unemployment rate was moderately less than it was in 1965. At the same time, the nonwhite contribution to the labor force grew from 10.7 per cent in 1956 to 11.1 per cent in 1965.

A few words are necessary about the tragic plight of nonwhite youth. The position of nonwhite (chiefly Negro) teen-agers in the labor market has deteriorated since World War II in two dramatic stages. These two periods are delineated in Table 6.7, supplemented by Table 6.1. Between 1948 and the end of the 1950's, unemployment rates for nonwhite teen-agers rose more rapidly than did those of white teen-agers; the relative deterioration was even more severe for teen-agers than for adult non-whites.[16] Moreover, as we have learned (Table 6.5), the relative position of the entire nonwhite labor force deteriorated seriously between 1948 and 1956; the overall nonwhite unemployment rate rose from about 1.5 times the national rate in 1948 to twice the national rate in 1956. The unemployment rate for nonwhite teen-agers rose even more on a relative basis.

Since 1959 the position of nonwhite teenagers in the labor market has deteriorated still further, but chiefly because the position of all teen-agers has deteriorated. The ratio of nonwhite to white unemployment rates in the teen-age group did not show a significant increase between 1959 and 1965, for either males or females (Table 6.7); indeed, for 18- and 19-year-olds of both sexes there was some slight *relative* improvement, compared to the same white age group, during this more recent period. (This gain was lost when the relative position of this nonwhite age group worsened significantly in 1966.) However, as we observed

TABLE 6.7.   Ratio of Nonwhite to White Unemployment Rates by Age Groups, Ages 14 to 24, for Selected Years, 1948-1965.

Year	Males			Females		
	14–19	18–19 only	20–24	14–19	18–19 only	20–24
1948	1.0	1.1	1.8	1.5	2.1	2.4
1953	1.1	1.1	1.8	1.3	1.7	1.3
1956	1.6	1.5	2.0	2.3	2.8	2.9
1959	1.8	2.1	2.2	2.3	2.7	2.2
1960	1.7	1.9	1.6	1.9	2.1	2.1
1961	1.8	1.6	1.5	2.0	2.1	2.3
1962	1.7	1.7	1.8	2.5	2.8	2.4
1963	1.8	1.9	2.0	2.4	2.4	2.5
1964	1.7	1.7	1.7	2.3	2.2	2.6
1965	1.9	1.8	1.6	2.4	2.1	2.2

Source: Computed from data in Manpower Report of the President, March 1966, Statistical Appendix.

earlier, the position of teenagers as a group, white and nonwhite combined, deteriorated seriously in the first half of the 1960's.

The net result of these trends has been to yield the shockingly high unemployment rates for nonwhite teen-agers that were reported in 1965—22.6 per cent for boys and 29.8 per cent for girls, compared to the comparable rates for whites of 11.8 and 12.6 per cent, respectively. The rate for nonwhite girls had been as high as 33.1 per cent in 1963.

The relative worsening in the position of the nonwhite 20–24 age group in the first postwar decade was less serious than that of teen-agers, and, relative to whites, some noticeable improvement has occurred since 1956. For this reason, as indicated in Table 6.7, in 1965 nonwhites aged 20 to 24 were less badly off, compared to whites in the same age group, than they were in 1948 or 1956. However, this was still consistent with 1965 unemployment rates in this age group of 9.3 per cent for males and 13.7 per cent for females, compared to corresponding rates for whites of 5.9 and 6.3 per cent.

We need to consider now the possibility that our analysis of nonwhite unemployment trends may be subject to an important modification because of the presumed increase in disguised unemployment among nonwhites. Labor-force participation rates for nonwhite adult males have been declining, and more rapidly than those for the corresponding white age groups. Do our earlier findings still hold if an appropriate allowance is made for the presumed increase in disguised unemployment resulting from the drop in labor force participation rates? An attempt was made to answer this question, at least partially, in the following way.

Taking 1956 as a base year, we compared the decline in labor force participation rates for white males with the comparable decline for nonwhite males from 1956 to 1959 and from 1956 to 1965. The excess of the decline in the nonwhite over the white participation rate since 1956 was added to the reported nonwhite participation rate in 1959 and in 1965. These calculations were performed separately for each 10-year age group from 25 to 64.[17] These "adjusted" participation rates were then used to calculate new estimates of the labor force in each of the age groups in 1959 and in 1965. The excess of the adjusted over the original reported labor force figure in each case was also added to reported unemployment. In this way we added a rough estimate of the increase since 1956 in disguised unemployment among nonwhite adult males (relative to white males) to the unemployment actually reported for this group in the years 1959 and 1965. The effect of these calculations on our measure $(U_i/U - L_i/L)$ is indicated by the following tabulation.

	$U_i/U - L_i/L$ (per cent)		
Sector	1956	1959	1965
Nonwhite males, 25–64			
Unadjusted	3.2	3.8	1.0
Adjusted	—	4.2	2.2
All nonwhite males			
Unadjusted	6.0	7.2	4.4
Adjusted	—	7.6	5.6

The adjustment for disguised unemployment does not wipe out the improvement since 1959 discovered when we used the data for only reported unemployment. Our measure $(U_i/U - L_i/L)$ is lower in 1965 than in 1956 or 1959, even when our allowance for declining labor-force participation among adult nonwhite males is added to recorded unemployment. This is true for the 25–64 age group alone, and it is also true if we adjust our measure for all nonwhite males by adding disguised unemployment in the 25–64 group.

Distribution of Unemployment by Occupation

We turn now to an occupational breakdown of the unemployed (Table 6.8). It is fair to state that all variants of the hypothesis, that the structural element in total unemployment has become more serious over the last decade, imply that unemployment has come to be increasingly concentrated among blue-collar and unskilled workers.[18] These (along with relatively unskilled service workers) are the occupational groups in which unemployment rates tend to be higher than the national average. To the extent that unemployment has in fact tended to become more concentrated among unskilled and semiskilled blue-collar workers, we should expect to find that our relative dispersion index would have shown a significant rise since the mid-1950's.

As the two last lines of Table 6.8 demonstrate, this has not, in fact, happened. To show what has happened, we must look at two variants of our dispersion index: one which includes those with no previous work experience (who by definition do not have an occupational attachment) and a second variant which excludes this group.

We shall consider first the version of the dispersion index which includes those with no previous work experience (last line of Table 6.8). This measure reached a postwar low in 1953, rose sharply until 1956, and since then has shown little further change. Our index in 1965 (with a national unemployment rate of 4.6 per cent) was almost the same as that in 1956 (with an unemployment rate of 4.2 per cent).

A careful look at Table 6.8 reveals that the horizontal movement of the dispersion index over the last decade is the result of two striking developments which have been working in opposite directions. Since 1953, this country has been experiencing a dramatic increase in the proportion of the unemployed who have had no previous work experience. In our terms this represents a significant structural worsening. At the same time, however, the fraction of total unemployment accounted for by unskilled and semiskilled blue-collar workers has declined markedly, particularly since 1959. The decline in the relative importance of blue-collar unemployment is reflected in the behavior of our dispersion index when those with no previous work experience are excluded. (See the next to last line in Table 6.8.) This variant of D_u was substantially lower in 1965 than in 1956. Indeed, the 1965 figure was the smallest for the entire postwar period.

Let us now examine the unemployment record for the different occupational groups listed in Table 6.8. With respect to white-collar workers, the postwar years clearly fall into two periods. In the first, from 1948 to 1956, the relative position of the white-collar group as a whole, which was already very favorable, improved still further. The unemployment rate for this sector of the labor force fell from 60 to 45 per cent of the national rate; and, although its share of the labor force increased, it accounted for a significantly smaller fraction of total unemployment in 1956 than in 1948. With minor exceptions, the same trends held for the subgroups listed under the white-collar heading.

Now we shall discuss the surprising reversal that seems to have occurred since 1956. The white-collar unemployment rate, while still remaining relatively low, has actually worsened moderately relative to the national rate; and this deterioration, combined with the continued rise in this sector's share of the total labor force, has meant that white-collar workers in 1965 made up a significantly larger fraction of total unemployment than in 1956. Again, all of the component groups shared in these changes.

Let us now inspect the blue-collar occupations listed in Table 6.8. For all the blue-collar workers together, the relative unemployment rate worsened only at the beginning of the postwar period, between 1948 and 1953, and this was the period in which the national unemployment rate fell to the lowest figure it reached during the entire postwar period. Since 1953, the blue-collar relative rate has not worsened. At the same time, the blue-collar fraction of the total labor force has continued its steady decline. As a result, blue-collar workers comprised a significantly smaller fraction of total unemployment in 1965 than a decade earlier. The bulk of this improvement occurred in the 1960's. Between 1959 and 1965 our measure $(U_i/U - L_i/L)$ for the blue-collar group declined sharply, from 14.2 per cent to 5.6 per cent.

On the whole, these same trends are reflected in the different subgroups of blue-collar workers shown in Table 6.8. The deterioration in the relative unemployment rate for semiskilled operatives continued until 1956 rather than 1953, but it has declined significantly since then. Indeed, by 1965 the relative unemployment rate for this group was as low as it had been in the entire postwar period—and its contribution to total unemployment was the lowest that it had been since the war. The figures for unskilled laborers are particularly striking. Their relative unemployment rate in 1965, at 1.83, was at a postwar low. (In only one earlier year, in 1951, had this figure fallen below 2.00.)

TABLE 6.8. Occupational Classification of the Civilian Labor Force and the Unemployed, Selected Years, 1948-1965

Occupation	1948			1953			1956			1959			1965		
	A	B	C	A	B	C	A	B	C	A	B	C	A	B	C
White-collar	0.60	35.5	21.6	0.56	37.8	20.5	0.45	38.6	17.5	0.47	41.2	19.3	0.50	43.4	21.7
Professional, technical	0.50	6.6	3.4	0.36	8.7	3.0	0.26	9.1	2.4	0.31	10.5	3.2	0.33	11.9	3.8
Managers, officials, proprietors	0.29	10.4	3.3	0.36	10.2	3.8	0.21	9.8	2.0	0.24	10.1	2.4	0.24	9.8	2.4
Clerical	0.68	12.4	8.6	0.68	12.8	8.5	0.63	13.4	8.6	0.67	14.0	9.3	0.70	15.3	10.8
Sales	1.00	6.1	6.3	0.84	6.1	5.2	0.71	6.3	4.5	0.67	6.6	4.4	0.72	6.4	4.7
Blue-collar	1.26	40.8	52.0	1.38	40.8	55.8	1.34	39.3	52.6	1.38	37.7	51.9	1.15	36.9	42.5
Craftsmen, foremen	0.85	13.6	12.0	1.04	13.9	14.5	0.84	13.3	11.3	0.96	13.0	12.5	0.78	12.6	9.9
Operatives	1.21	21.1	26.0	1.28	20.8	26.5	1.42	20.1	28.5	1.38	18.5	25.5	1.20	18.7	22.4
Laborers	2.21	6.1	14.0	2.44	6.1	14.8	2.16	5.9	12.8	2.25	6.2	13.9	1.83	5.6	10.2
Service	1.31	10.3	13.6	1.33	11.4	15.0	1.21	11.8	14.5	1.09	12.3	13.4	1.13	13.0	14.8
Household workers	0.94	3.0	2.9	1.00	3.0	3.0	1.11	3.3	3.6	0.87	3.3	2.9	0.91	3.1	2.9
Others	1.41	7.3	10.7	1.44	8.4	12.0	1.26	8.5	10.9	1.16	9.0	10.5	1.20	9.9	11.9

	A	B	C	A	B	C	A	B	C	A	B	C	A	B	C
Farm	0.31	13.0	4.2	0.45	10.0	4.4	0.50	9.8	4.9	0.45	8.3	3.8	0.57	5.8	3.3
Farmers and farm managers	0.06	7.6	0.4	0.08	6.1	0.6	0.11	5.4	0.5	0.05	4.4	0.2	0.09	3.0	0.3
Farm laborers and foremen	0.68	5.4	3.8	1.00	3.9	3.8	0.97	4.4	4.4	0.93	3.9	3.6	1.04	2.8	3.0
No previous work experience	---	0.3	8.8	---	0.1	4.4	---	0.4	10.4	---	0.6	11.6	---	0.8	17.7
National unemployment rate [a] (per cent)		3.8 (3.4)			2.9 (2.5)			4.2 (3.8)			5.5			4.6	
Relative dispersion index [b] (excluding NPWE) [c]		0.410			0.415			0.460			0.435			0.378	
(including NPWE) [c]		0.495			0.458			0.560			0.545			0.547	

Source: Manpower Report of the President, March 1966, Statistical Appendix.

[a] The national unemployment rates for 1956 and earlier years shown on this line have been adjusted to reflect changes in definitions adopted subsequently. The figures in parentheses are the unadjusted rates which are consistent with the individual rates for the various groups shown here. The unrevised national rate was used in the calculations for 1956 and prior years.

[b] This measure is explained in detail in Chapter 5. It is the sum of the absolute differences between the fraction of total unemployment and the fraction of the total civilian labor force accounted for by each group.

[c] NPWE stands for those with no previous work experience.

Column headings:

A. Ratio of group's unemployment rate to national unemployment rate.

B. Percentage of civilian labor force in each group.

C. Percentage of total unemployment in each group.

The group constituted a smaller proportion of total unemployment in 1965 than in any of the earlier years presented in Table 6.7; again, this percentage was at a postwar low.[19]

The service group provides a rather different situation. The relative unemployment rate for this group, whose share of the labor force has been steadily rising, declined during the 1950's, but there was a slight increase between 1959 and 1965. The same trends appear when we examine the fraction of total unemployment: a decline from 1953 to 1959 and an increase to 1965. This moderate relative deterioration since 1959 is more clearly revealed if we exclude household workers. It would appear that, insofar as there has been some relative worsening since the late 1950's in the position of the less skilled and less educated with some previous work experience, this worsening shows up among service workers rather than among unskilled laborers and semi-skilled operatives. Of course, this may reflect to some extent the fact that formerly unemployed blue-collar workers have moved into the more routine service occupations and, when counted as unemployed in, say, 1965, reported that their last previous employment had been in a service job.

We can quickly review the farm group. As in the case of service workers, the relative unemployment rate for farm workers declined from 1953 to 1959 and then rose moderately until 1965. With the rapid decline in this sector's share of the labor force, its share of total unemployment was significantly lower in 1965 than in any of the other years shown in Table 6.8.[20]

First-Job Seekers

We must now inspect more closely the final category listed in Table 6.8. The fraction of total unemployment made up of those with no previous work experience, after falling sharply between 1948 and 1953, quadrupled between 1953 and 1965. "No previous work experience" refers to people looking for their first job. Naturally, these would be either youths in school or fresh out of school (or military service) or married women entering the labor force for the first time.

It appears that in this case we need to look at the unbroken

TABLE 6.9. Percentage of the Unemployed Having No Previous Work Experience, 1947-1965

Year	Percentage	Year	Percentage
1947	9.4	1957	10.3
1948	8.8	1958	9.3
1949	6.6	1959	11.6
1950	6.8	1960	11.6
1951	7.3	1961	12.2
1952	8.3	1962	13.4
1953	4.4	1963	14.8
1954	7.0	1964	16.0
1955	8.4	1965	17.7
1956	10.4		

Source: Manpower Report of the President, March 1966, Statistical Appendix.

series of annual figures and not merely at those for the years in which unemployment reached its cyclical lows. The full set of annual data is presented in Table 6.9. It is apparent that 1953 represents somewhat of an aberration.[21] Excluding this year, we can say that the percentage of total unemployment made up of first-job seekers declined rather sharply in the late forties, fluctuated around a horizontal trend until 1954, and then began to move up rather persistently. By 1956, the percentage already was higher than it had been in any previous postwar year; and it rose further from 10.4 to 17.7 between 1956 and 1965. The rise was particularly rapid after 1960.

The lessened importance of first-job seekers in the late forties seems to be associated with a sharp drop in the contribution of the male 20–24 age group to total unemployment. These young men accounted for 16.6 per cent of unemployment in 1947, and this percentage dropped each year until it was as low as 7.4 in 1951, after which it began slowly to rise again. In addition to demographic factors, this downward trend undoubtedly reflected the absorption into the job market of young veterans after completion of their education and training.

The sharp rise since 1960 in the proportion of the unemployed without previous work experience is undoubtedly due chiefly to the rapid rise in the teen-age portions of total unemployment, particularly since 1962. According to Table 6.9, the fraction of unemployment accounted for by those with no previous job experience rose by 6.1 percentage points between 1960 and 1965. During the same five years, the teen-age share rose by 7.9 percentage points; the 20–24 age group increased its quota by only 1.3 percentage points; and the percentage of total unemployment accounted for by women 25 and older rose only 1.5 points. It does not appear that mature women entering the labor force accounted for much, if any, of the recent rapid increase in the proportion of the unemployed accounted for by persons without previous job experience. This increase in the last five years or so seems to be chiefly another manifestation of the relative worsening of the teen-age unemployment problem.

It would seem that the burden of the deteriorating job market between the mid-fifties and the early 1960's fell relatively more heavily on those seeking their first job than on experienced (including even manual) workers. Such structural changes as have occurred have not resulted in a (relatively) growing pool of experienced blue-collar workers who cannot find new jobs. A variety of forms of job security tend to protect the experienced worker, and the gradual reduction in the proportions of the labor force employed in certain occupations and industries has been effected in good part through natural attrition (retirement, death, and voluntary quits) rather than through wholesale lay-offs. It has, as a result, become increasingly difficult for new entrants into the labor force to find their first job.[22] It is worth noting, also, that, at least until 1960 or so, the relative increase in the number of first-job seekers among the unemployed represented young adults, both men and women, as much as it did teen-agers. This situation seems to have changed radically since 1960, particularly since 1962, when the teen-age portion of total employment began to rise rapidly.

Another consideration that is relevant here has recently been put forward by Edward Kalachek in a perceptive paper.[23] A given overall unemployment rate maintained for some time will yield a different pattern of unemployment than will the same rate experienced for a short period as the economy moves to lower or higher unemployment levels during the course of the business cycle. A 5 per cent rate achieved as the economy moves down from full employment into a recession will reflect a large number of layoffs, a good many of them adult males in blue-collar jobs. However, if the economy grows steadily at a moderate pace that leaves the unemployment rate more or less unchanged at 5 per cent, experienced workers will be rehired and the unemployed will come increasingly to consist of new entrants into the labor force and recent voluntary quits—that is, predominantly women and youths. Also, unemployment will be less concentrated among workers attached to cyclically sensitive industries (that is, durable-goods manufacturing) than was true when the same overall rate of unemployment was experienced during cyclical recessions and recoveries.

This hypothesis is consistent with some of our findings regarding the pattern of unemployment during the first half of the 1960's; not only the deteriorating position of teen-agers and others without previous work experience but also the marked improvement in the position of semiskilled operatives and workers in (particularly durable-goods) manufacturing. However, it is obviously not the whole story. It does not explain the fact that the position of the inexperienced and of women under 45 worsened somewhat during the 1950's as well as after 1961, and it does not account for the other changes in the incidence of unemployment that we found before 1956. Nor can we neglect the changes in the pattern of labor supply that we have emphasized, that is, the accelerated inflow of teen-agers into the labor market in the early sixties and the continued rise in female labor force participation.

Unemployment by Industry

We need not spend much time on the distribution of unemployment by industry, as presented in Table 6.10. We are already familiar with one fact brought out by the table: the decline, particularly since 1959, in the fraction of total unemployment accounted for by experienced workers. Whatever the impact of

TABLE 6.10. Industrial Classification of the Civilian Labor Force and the Unemployed, Selected Years, 1948–1965

Industry	1948			1953			1956			1959			1965		
	A	B^c	C	A	B^c	C	A	B^c	C	A	B^c	C	A	B^c	C
Experienced wage and salary earners	1.09	80.6	87.7	1.08	82.0	88.6	1.03	83.6	85.8	1.02	84.1	85.6	0.91	87.1	79.5
Agriculture	1.38	3.0	4.2	1.88	2.4	4.5	1.71	2.7	4.6	1.58	2.7	4.2	1.59	2.1	3.4
Nonagricultural industries	1.09	76.7	83.5	1.04	80.9	84.1	1.00	81.2	81.2	1.00	81.4	81.4	0.91	83.4	76.1
Mining, forestry, fisheries	0.85	1.6	1.4	1.96	1.4	2.7	1.68	1.2	2.1	1.76	1.0	1.8	1.20	0.8	1.0
Construction	2.24	4.8	10.7	2.44	5.3	12.9	2.18	5.4	11.8	2.18	5.8	12.6	1.96	5.6	10.9
Manufacturing	1.03	27.2	28.0	1.00	27.0	27.0	1.11	26.2	29.0	1.09	25.5	27.8	0.87	25.9	22.5
Durables	1.00	14.3	14.3	0.80	16.4	13.1	1.05	15.3	16.1	1.11	14.5	16.1	0.74	15.0	11.1
Nondurables	1.06	12.8	13.6	1.24	11.2	13.9	1.16	11.1	12.9	1.07	10.8	11.6	1.00	11.4	11.4
Transportation and public utilities	0.88	7.7	6.8	0.72	7.4	5.3	0.63	7.1	4.5	0.76	6.5	5.0	0.59	6.3	3.7
Wholesale and retail	1.26	14.9	18.8	1.20	14.9	17.9	1.08	15.4	16.6	1.05	15.5	16.3	1.09	15.7	17.1

	A	B	C	A	B	C	A	B	C	A	B	C	A	B	C
Finance, insurance, real estate	0.47	2.8	1.3	0.64	3.0	1.9	0.37	3.3	1.2	0.47	3.6	1.7	0.50	4.2	2.1
Service industries	1.03	13.5	13.9	0.96	14.7	14.1	0.84	16.9	14.2	0.78	18.3	14.3	0.83	20.3	16.8
Public administration	0.59	4.6	2.7	0.48	4.6	2.2	0.42	4.5	1.9	0.42	4.5	1.9	0.41	5.1	2.1
National unemployment rate[a] (per cent)	3.8 (3.4)			2.9 (2.5)			4.2 (3.8)			5.5			4.6		
Relative dispersion index[b]	0.167			0.262			0.230			0.223			0.233		

SOURCE: Manpower Report of the President, March 1966, Statistical Appendix.

[a]The national unemployment rates for 1956 and earlier years shown on this line have been adjusted to reflect changes in definitions adopted subsequently. The figures in parentheses are the unadjusted rates which are consistent with the individual rates for the various groups shown here. The unrevised national rate was used in the calculations for 1956 and prior years.

[b]This measure is explained in detail in Chapter 5. It is the sum of the absolute differences between the fraction of total unemployment and the fraction of the total civilian labor force accounted for by each group.

[c]The percentages of the labor force in this column were obtained by dividing Column C by Column A. As a result, some of the rounding errors are not insignificant.

Column headings:

  A. Ratio of group's unemployment rate to national unemployment rate.

  B. Percentage of civilian labor force in each group.

  C. Percentage of total unemployment in each group.

technological change in other respects, as far as unemployment is concerned, it is not the experienced worker as much as the new job seeker who has chiefly suffered.

Our dispersion measure, which is based on an industry classification of wage and salary workers only, was virtually the same in 1965 as in 1956 and 1959. The increase in this index occurred early in the postwar period, between 1948 and 1953.

In the debate in the early 1960's regarding the possibility of increasing structural unemployment, it was widely assumed that technological change was tending to push up unemployment rates particularly in manufacturing, transportation, and public utilities, and to increase the proportion of total unemployment accounted for by these sectors. This is not the story we get from Table 6.10, at least for the years since 1956 or 1959. It is true that the portions of employment and of the labor force accounted for by these industries has shown some decline over the postwar period, but unemployment rates in these sectors have not risen relatively, and their share of total unemployment has, since the mid-1950's, declined more than their share of the

TABLE 6.11. Changing Pattern of Unemployment Among Industrial Sectors

Industry	Relative Unemployment Rate			$U_i/U - L_i/L$ (per cent)[a]		
	1948	1956	1965	1948	1956	1965
Construction	2.24	2.18	1.96	5.9	6.4	5.3
Manufacturing						
Durables	1.00	1.05	.74	0.0	0.8	-3.9
Nondurables	1.06	1.16	1.00	0.8	1.8	0.0
Transportation and public utilities	0.88	0.63	0.59	-0.9	-2.6	-2.6
Subtotal				5.8	6.4	-1.2
Trade	1.26	1.08	1.09	3.9	1.2	1.4
Finance, insurance, real estate	0.47	0.37	0.50	-1.5	-2.1	-2.1
Service	1.03	0.84	0.83	0.4	-2.7	-3.5
Public administration	0.59	0.42	0.41	-1.9	-2.6	-3.0
Subtotal				0.9	-6.2	-7.2

Source: Table 6.10.

[a]Difference between each sector's share of total unemployment and of the total labor force.

labor force. These trends are summarized in Table 6.11, which is derived from Table 6.10.

As Table 6.11 reveals, the relative unemployment rate in manufacturing showed a net decline between 1956 and 1965, particularly in durables. And whereas in 1948 and 1956 manufacturing accounted for a larger fraction of unemployment than it did of the labor force, the reverse was true in 1965. Our measure $(U_i/U - L_i/L)$ rose for both manufacturing and construction between 1948 and 1956, but it declined in both sectors between 1956 and 1965. In the trade, financial-real estate, service, and government sectors, we find little further relative improvement between 1956 and 1965, in contrast to the marked decline in relative unemployment rates and in $(U_i/U - L_i/L)$ which occurred between 1948 and 1956.

Insofar as technical change ("automation" and the like) and the changing composition of demand for goods and services have created a structural worsening in the pattern of unemployment, this worsening took place *before* 1956, not after. This is the conclusion that emerges from our study of both occupational and industry patterns of unemployment. Such structural worsening in unemployment patterns as occurred between the mid-fifties and mid-sixties resulted chiefly from changes on the *supply* side of the labor market, particularly from changes in the age-sex composition of the labor force.[24]

Education and Unemployment

One variant of the thesis that structural unemployment has been worsening emphasizes the deteriorating position of those with relatively little education.[25] There is no question that the incidence of unemployment is inversely related to the level of education, as is clearly revealed in Table 6.12. However, the evidence does not suggest that, at least during the last decade or so, unemployment has come to be more heavily concentrated among those with the least schooling.[26]

We shall first inspect our relative dispersion index (last line of Table 6.12). This measure rose significantly between 1950 and 1959, but it then showed a moderate decline to 1965.[27]

TABLE 6.12. Educational Classification of the Civilian Labor Force and the Unemployed, 18 Years and Over, by Sex, Selected Years, 1950–1965

Educational attainment and sex	April 1950[a]			March 1957[c]			March 1959			March 1962			March 1965		
	A	B	C	A	B	C	A	B	C	A	B	C	A	B	C
Males															
Total	1.02	71.9	73.6	1.00	67.9	67.6	1.02	67.2	67.9	1.00	66.2	66.2	0.94	65.0	60.7
0–4 years	1.38	6.9	9.7	1.95	4.8	9.5	1.60	4.1	6.6	1.73	3.6	6.2	1.51	2.9	4.3
5–8 years	1.21	25.7	31.0	1.24	19.8	25.0	1.34	18.1	24.3	1.32	16.0	21.3	1.21	13.8	16.6
9–11 years	1.15	13.7	15.8	1.15	13.3	15.4	1.31	13.6	17.7	1.30	13.0	17.0	1.43	12.6	18.0
12 years	0.77	15.3	11.7	0.73	17.8	13.0	0.79	18.3	14.4	0.80	19.0	15.2	0.72	20.8	14.9
13–15 years	0.68	5.3	3.6	0.66	5.6	3.8	0.53	6.1	3.3	0.67	6.9	4.6	0.66	6.8	4.5
16 years or more	0.38	5.1	1.8	0.15	6.5	1.0	0.23	7.0	1.6	0.23	7.7	1.9	0.30	8.1	2.5
Females															
Total	0.94	28.1	26.4	1.00	32.1	32.4	0.98	32.8	32.1	1.00	33.8	33.8	1.13	35.0	39.3
0–4 years	1.47	1.6	2.3	1.63	1.4	2.2	1.66	1.2	1.9	1.25	1.0	1.3	1.89	0.8	1.6
5–8 years	1.21	7.3	8.9	1.34	7.3	10.0	1.26	7.0	8.9	1.15	6.4	7.3	1.15	5.8	6.6
9–11 years	1.26	5.2	6.6	1.44	6.1	8.8	1.50	6.3	9.4	1.53	6.4	9.8	1.83	6.6	11.9
12 years	0.70	8.9	6.3	0.71	11.7	8.4	0.76	12.5	9.4	0.95	13.1	12.5	1.06	14.7	15.5
13–15 years	0.55	2.8	1.6	0.78	3.0	2.4	0.61	3.2	1.9	0.53	3.8	2.0	0.77	3.6	2.7
16 years or more	0.30	2.2	0.7	0.24	2.7	0.7	0.21	2.7	0.5	0.25	3.2	0.8	0.28	3.5	1.0

144

National unemployment rate	6.1 (4.7)	4.1	6.2	6.0	4.7
Relative dispersion[b] index	0.278	0.362	0.372	0.332	0.345

Sources: 1950: U. S. Bureau of the Census, 1950 U. S. Census of Population. Special Report PE No. 5B, "Education," p. 73, Table 9.

1957: U. S. Bureau of the Census Current Population Reports--Labor Force Series, P-50, No. 78, "Educational Attainment of Workers: March 1957," November 1957, p. 8, Table 1.

1959, 1962, 1965: U. S. Bureau of Labor Statistics, Special Labor Force Reports, Nos. 1, 30 and 65, "Education Attainment of Workers."

[a]The 1950 Census and the Current Population Survey of April 2-8, 1950, show important discrepancies with respect to the size of the labor force and the number of unemployed. The latter is generally regarded to be more accurate and more consistent with other estimates. However it does not provide a breakdown by educational attainment. Charles Killingsworth has made estimates of employment status by educational attainment by taking the proportions obtained from the Census enumeration and applying them to the higher totals found by the CPS. His estimate of total unemployment is 6.1 per cent compared to the 4.7 per cent obtained by the Census enumeration.

The figures shown here are calculated directly from the Census figures. However, except for slight rounding errors, they give the same results as Killingsworth's revised figures because the numerator and the denominator of each ratio are multiplied by the same constant for Killingsworth's estimates.

[b]This measure is explained in detail in Chapter 5. It is the sum of the absolute differences between the fraction of total unemployment and the fraction of the labor force (18 years and over) accounted for by each group.

[c]Column headings:

  A. Ratio of group's unemployment rate to national unemployment rate.

  B. Percentage of civilian labor force in each group.

  C. Percentage of total unemployment in each group.

Relative unemployment rates clearly worsened between 1950 and 1957 for those with eight or fewer years of education of both sexes. Since 1957, relative unemployment rates have shown some improvement for males with no more than four years of education, and there has been no further worsening in the rate for those with five to eight years of schooling.[28] In the case of women, relative unemployment rates showed a net rise between 1957 and 1965 for those with no more than four years of education and a small decline for those with from five to eight years of schooling.[29] *Relative* unemployment rates between 1957 and 1965 also rose for high school dropouts of both sexes (9–11 years of education), for female high school graduates, and even for those with four or more years of college, particularly males.

Much more important than these trends in relative unemployment rates has been the changing educational pattern of the labor force and of unemployment. The average educational level of the labor force has been steadily rising. In 1965, only 24.3 per cent of the male and 17.8 per cent of the female labor force 18 to 64 years old had a grammar school education or less, compared to percentages of, respectively, 34.5 and 25.8 in 1957

TABLE 6.13. Differences Between Percentage Shares of Unemployment and of the Labor Force, 18 Years Old and Over, by Educational Attainment, 1950-1965

Educational attainment and sex	1950	1957	1959	1962	1965
Males					
0–8 years	8.1	9.9	8.7	7.9	4.2
9–11 years	2.1	2.1	4.1	4.0	5.4
12 years	-3.6	-4.8	-3.9	-3.8	-5.9
13–15 years	-1.7	-1.8	-2.8	-2.3	-2.3
16 years or more	-3.3	-5.5	-5.4	-5.8	-5.6
Females					
0–8 years	2.3	3.5	2.6	1.2	1.6
9–11 years	1.4	2.7	3.1	3.4	5.3
12 years	-2.6	-3.3	-3.1	-0.6	0.8
13–15 years	-1.2	-0.6	-1.3	-1.8	-0.9
16 years or more	-1.5	-2.0	-2.2	-2.4	-2.5

Source: Table 6.12.

and 39.3 and 30.2 in 1952. In 1965, 58.7 per cent of the civilian labor force aged 18 and over had finished high school, compared to 48.5 per cent in 1957 and 44.4 per cent in 1952.[30]

What about the pattern of unemployment? If we take both sexes together, Table 6.12 indicates that, in 1957, 70.9 per cent of the unemployed had less than 12 years of schooling. This figure had fallen to 59 per cent by 1965. Those with only a grammar school education or less accounted for 46.7 per cent of total unemployment in 1957, but for only 29.1 per cent in 1965. The group whose proportion of total unemployment has risen the most is that of female high school graduates; it accounted for 8.4 per cent of total adult unemployment in 1957 but for as much as 15.5 per cent in 1965. Taking both sexes together, we see that the fraction of total adult unemployment accounted for by those with some college education rose from 7.9 per cent in 1957 to 10.7 per cent in 1965.

Table 6.13 presents our measure $(U_i/U - L_i/L)$ for the different levels of education. At least five important conclusions can be drawn from the figures there presented:

1. As we already know, education makes a tremendous difference in one's vulnerability to unemployment.

2. This association between education and unemployment is more pronounced for males than for females.

3. The *relative* position of those with only a grammar school education has actually improved since 1957, but that of high school dropouts has worsened.

4. In terms of our measure, a significant increase in relative vulnerability to unemployment has occurred among female high school graduates, for whom $(U_i/U - L_i/L)$ rose from —3.3 to 0.8 per cent between 1957 and 1965.

5. The favorable relative position of college graduates, which improved between 1950 and 1957, showed no further improvement after 1957. Indeed, the relative unemployment rate and fraction of total unemployment rose for college graduates, more so for males than females[31] (Table 6.12).

With education, as well as along the other labor force dimensions that we have considered, we must ask to what extent our conclusions need to be modified because of a growing amount of disguised unemployment among those groups with the highest unemployment rates. Labor force participation rates among those with a grammar school education or less have shown a marked decline over the postwar period—much more of a decline than for those who have finished high school.[32] To what extent is this decline in participation rates to be attributed to the inability to find jobs, and how much are our results modified by a reasonable allowance for this increase in disguised unemployment?

An estimate of disguised unemployment is never easy to make. It is particularly difficult here because of the interrelationship between age and education. With the marked upward trend in the level of education, the average age of the least educated tends to rise with the passing years. Some part of the decline in the participation rate of those with eight or fewer years of schooling unquestionably reflects the range of forces which lead older persons generally to retire from the labor force. This is not to deny that there has probably been some increase in disguised unemployment associated with the handicaps resulting from little education. However, recent research suggests that our conclusions still hold even if a fairly generous allowance is made for increasing disguised unemployment among the least educated.[33] To the extent that there was a significant increase in structural unemployment among the least educated, it occurred before rather than after 1957. The structural worsening that has occurred since then has affected chiefly high school dropouts and women who have graduated from high school.

Long-Term Unemployment

A few words should be said about long-term unemployment, the reduction in which should certainly be one of the major goals of employment and manpower policy.[34] As Table 6.14 displays in striking fashion, those out of work 15 (or 26) weeks or more make up a substantially larger fraction of total unemployment now than in the early postwar years. Here again, however, the deterioration occurred chiefly in the 1950's rather than the 1960's. If we compare years of cyclical peak employment, the increase in the incidence of long-term unemployment occurred chiefly between 1953 and 1956 and between 1956 and

TABLE 6.14.   The Relative Importance of Long-Term Unemployment, 1947–1965

| Year | Percentage of Unemployed Out of Work 15 Weeks or Longer | | |
	Total	15–26 Weeks	27 Weeks and Over
1948	13.3	8.3	5.0
1953	11.3	7.1	4.2
1956	18.9	10.7	8.2
1959	27.3	12.3	15.0
1960	24.3	12.8	11.5
1961	31.9	15.1	16.7
1962	27.9	13.3	14.6
1963	26.1	12.8	13.3
1964	25.1	12.6	12.4
1965	21.8	11.7	10.2

Source: Manpower Report of the President, March 1966, p. 171.

1959. (We must remember, however, that the national unemployment rate also rose during this period, from 2.9 per cent in 1953 to 4.2 per cent in 1956 and 5.5 per cent in 1959.) Some net deterioration occurred between 1956 and 1965. Those unemployed 15 weeks or longer increased from 18.9 to 21.8 per cent of total unemployment, and those out of work more than 26 weeks rose from 8.2 to 10.2 per cent of all unemployed. We should also note the marked improvement which occurred between 1961 and 1965, largely as a result of the decline in the overall unemployment rate.

Table 6.15 gives us some basis for judging whether the incidence of long-term unemployment has changed significantly since the 1950's. Compared to the pattern of total unemployment, long-term unemployment is concentrated particularly among males aged 45–64, among nonwhite males, and, to a moderate degree, among semiskilled operatives and unskilled laborers. In none of these groups did long-term unemployment become a significantly larger fraction of total unemployment between 1957 and 1965. In general, changes in the distribution of long-term

TABLE 6.15.   Percentage Distribution of Total and Long-Term (15 Weeks or More) Unemployment by Age, Sex, Color and Occupation, 1957-1965

Classification	1957 Total	1957 Long-term	1959 Total	1959 Long-term	1961 Total	1961 Long-term	1965 Total	1965 Long-term
By age and sex								
Male, total								
18–19	5.4	4.1	5.4	4.4	5.4	4.1	6.7	4.9
25–44	22.3	22.0	23.3	26.4	22.7	25.0	16.7	18.3
45–64	17.8	25.7	17.8	22.9	17.6	22.8	13.7	21.1
Female, total								
18–19	3.6	2.7	3.8	2.3	4.3	2.7	6.7	5.2
25–44	14.3	13.2	13.3	11.1	13.4	12.3	14.4	14.0
45–64	7.7	9.3	8.7	9.8	8.7	9.3	8.2	10.7
By color and sex								
White, total	80.1	77.4	78.8	75.7	79.5	77.5	79.7	77.0
Male	51.8	53.0	51.0	53.4	51.0	53.9	46.4	47.9
Female	28.3	24.4	27.8	22.4	28.5	23.6	33.3	29.2
Nonwhite, total	19.9	22.6	21.2	24.3	20.5	22.5	20.3	22.9
Male	12.7	15.8	13.8	17.9	12.7	15.3	10.9	13.0
Female	7.2	6.8	7.4	6.4	7.8	7.2	9.4	9.9
Selected occupations								
Clerical	9.2	8.2	9.3	9.4	9.9	9.8	10.8	10.3
Operatives	29.4	31.8	25.5	28.7	26.0	29.3	22.4	24.3
Service workers	10.2	10.6	10.5	10.3	10.5	10.6	11.9	12.5
Laborers	13.3	15.5	13.9	15.7	12.2	14.6	10.2	10.5
No previous work experience	10.3	8.4	11.6	8.8	12.2	9.2	17.7	13.8

Source: Manpower Report of the President, March 1966, pp. 172-174.

unemployment between 1957 and 1965 were very similar to the changes which occurred in the pattern of total unemployment. Long-term unemployment rose relative to total unemployment chiefly in the following instances: males aged 25–44, females aged 25–64, and nonwhite females. Interestingly, the last few lines of the table do not suggest any particular tendency for long-term unemployment to be increasingly concentrated among unskilled and semiskilled workers. In connection with all the groups mentioned, however, we must remember that we have made no allowance for possible increases in the relative importance of disguised unemployment, that is, withdrawal from the labor force because jobs are not available. Virtually by definition, disguised unemployment is long-term unemployment. That is, those who give up seeking work because no jobs are available are likely to be out of work for long periods.

A few conclusions may be drawn from this overly brief discussion. Long-term unemployment was a much more serious problem in 1965 than in the early postwar years when overall unemployment was below 4 per cent, and it was a slightly more important problem than it was in the mid-fifties, when the national unemployment rate was just about 4 per cent. Second, long-term unemployment clearly responds to a decline in total unemployment. The most important prescription to reduce long-term unemployment is the maintenance of a level of aggregate demand that will ensure a low level of total unemployment. However, beyond this, specific manpower measures are needed to reduce the incidence of protracted unemployment among particular groups: those over 45, nonwhites, and the less skilled. Such specific measures are needed not because these groups are much more prone to protracted unemployment now than a decade ago but because these are the groups upon which the incidence of long-term unemployment always falls most heavily.[35]

Some Other Matters

We have already considered at various points the extent to which our measurements based on recorded unemployment need to be modified to take account of disguised unemployment, that is, withdrawals from the labor force because jobs are not available. As we noted at the very end of Chapter 5, the same question arises with respect to involuntary part-time employment. A person who wants a full-time job but can find only 20 hours of work in a given week is listed as employed, not as half-unemployed.

The Bureau of Labor Statistics now makes monthly estimates of total labor force time lost through both complete unemployment and involuntary part-time unemployment. In 1965 this figure was 5.0 per cent, compared to the official unemployment rate of 4.6 per cent.

It would appear that involuntary part-time unemployment

was a relatively less important phenomenon in 1964–1965 than it was in 1956–1957. Thus the ratio of percentage of total labor force time lost to the unemployment rate was 1.21 in 1956 and 1.23 in 1957 but only 1.12 in 1964 and 1.09 in 1965.[36] Fewer persons were on part-time employment for economic reasons in 1965 than in 1957. Stated differently, persons on part-time for economic reasons were nearly two-thirds as numerous as those totally unemployed in each of the years 1963–1965, whereas in 1957 their number was about 85 per cent as large as officially recorded unemployment.

While involuntary part-time unemployment was thus a less serious problem in 1965 than in 1956–1957, there had been some changes in the composition of the group that worked only part-time because full-time jobs were not available. Compared to 1957, such involuntary part-time unemployment was more concentrated among males and females 18 to 24 years old, women aged 45–64, females generally, and (to a moderate extent) nonwhites. It was also much more concentrated in the trade and service industries in 1965 than in 1957.[37]

In raising questions regarding possible trends in disguised and involuntary part-time unemployment we were exploring the possibility that our dispersion measures did not fully reflect the structural changes that have occurred in the pattern of unemployment. We were concerned with the possibility that the position of some less advantaged groups had deteriorated more than was evident from the unemployment figures as they are regularly reported. On the whole, it would appear that our findings do not require substantial modification. So far as structural change is concerned our chief conclusions are:

1. Automation and changes in the composition of national output have not, since the mid-1950's, resulted in growing structural imbalance in the labor market affecting particularly unskilled and semiskilled blue-collar workers, nonwhites, or the least educated. Nor has unemployment come to be increasingly concentrated among manufacturing workers unable to move into other industries.[38]

2. The chief factor responsible for the high level of unemployment between 1958 and 1965 was an insufficiency of aggregate

demand. It has proved possible to get back to aggregative full employment at an overall unemployment rate of around 4 per cent without experiencing severe bottlenecks of skilled and educated workers and without an increasing concentration of unemployment among those presumably most affected by recent changes in technology and in the pattern of demand for final output.

3. Insofar as there was an increase in structural unemployment resulting from changes on the *demand* side of the labor market, this structural worsening occurred in the *first* postwar decade, not in the second. It was from the end of the war to the mid-1950's that we experienced a deterioration in the relative position of nonwhites, the least educated, and semiskilled blue-collar workers.

4. By our definition, some structural worsening has occurred since the mid-fifties, but it has come about primarily because of changes on the *supply* side of the labor market. These changes have been primarily two in number: (1) beginning in the early 1960's, the rapid increase in the number of young people entering the labor market, and (2) the steady increase in labor force participation rates for women.[39]

This last point raises a question that we have thus far not discussed. Most of us associate a greater loss of welfare with the unemployment of a husband and father who must support a family than with the unemployment of a married woman living with her husband or with that of a teen-ager even if he is no longer in school. That is, we believe that a given amount of unemployment withing the *primary* labor force involves a greater loss of welfare than the same amount of unemployment in the *secondary* labor force (chiefly married women living with their husbands and teen-agers living with their parents).

Our findings in this chapter suggest that a larger proportion of total unemployment is composed of secondary workers today than in the 1950's or earlier. Thus teen-agers made up 28 per cent of total unemployment in 1965 compared to 20 per cent in 1956 (Table 6.3). Or, to cite another comparison along the same lines, married males living with their wives constituted 35.5 per cent of total unemployment in March 1957 but only 29.1 per cent in the same month of 1965.[40] And in 1965 the unemployment rate for this group was lower relative to the national unemployment rate than it had been since 1952. This group's rate in 1965 (2.4 per cent) was only 52 per cent of the national rate. It ranged between 62 and 65 per cent of the national rate in 1955–1957, when the overall rate (4.2 to 4.4 per cent) was roughly comparable to that in 1965 (4.6 per cent).[41]

Here, we need to introduce a broader perspective. The blunt fact of the matter is that adult males (aged 25–64) have been declining as a fraction of the total labor force, and this trend will continue during the next decade.[42] Growth of the American economy is the resultant of the increase in the *total* labor force and the improvement in average productivity per worker—of the primary and the secondary labor force alike. To maintain the gratifying growth rate of the last few years, we must provide jobs for those who want to work in the secondary as well as in the primary labor force. Unemployment in both groups represents wasted resources and forgone output. This is apart from the enormous human and social problems created by high unemployment rates among youth of both sexes, not to mention the loss of welfare among families deprived of additional income because wives or sons or daughters who want to work cannot find jobs.

It is well to remember that so-called secondary workers make up a larger part of the labor force and of total unemployment today than a decade ago. But we should also remind ourselves that the nation suffers a serious loss in welfare (from each of several points of view) when recorded and disguised unemployment are larger among such groups than necessary. We need a policy of aggregative full employment that includes the secondary labor force, and we need also (at least by this author's evaluation of the costs and benefits involved) a manpower program that will significantly reduce structural unemployment among secondary as well as among primary workers. Again on the basis of one person's set of values, we urgently need a manpower program aimed particularly at the employment problems of youth, and, above all, at the employment problems of Negro youth. We also need, with only slightly less urgency, more effective programs than we now have to reduce relatively high unemployment rates wherever they are found. In this chapter there has been much discussion about who these high-unemployment groups are.

One final point should be stressed here. By the criteria we have used, the major structural worsening in unemployment patterns that has occurred in the last decade has involved the deteriorating position of youth, and, to a lesser extent, of women of all ages under 45. But the fact that the structural worsening in the labor market has not been even more widespread and serious should not blind us to what is perhaps the most important point of all. However much or little structural unemployment may have worsened in the last decade, it has always been a serious problem in the United States. Americans have belatedly awakened to the need for a vigorous manpower program not so much because structural unemployment has rapidly and markedly worsened in recent years but because of increasing social sensitivity to a problem that has always been with us. The recent and current efforts to cope with the depressingly high unemployment rates among Negroes is but one example of this. In an Affluent Society, structural unemployment and pockets of poverty seem less tolerable than was the case in earlier and less affluent times. It may seem to some a bit ironic that a number of other countries have needed less startling contrasts to initiate intensive manpower programs before the United States was prepared to develop means for coping with its own serious problems of structural unemployment.

NOTES

1. That is, the unemployment rates by age and sex which prevailed in 1956, given the distribution of the labor force in that year, resulted in an overall unemployment rate of 4.2 per cent. With the changed age-sex distribution of the labor force in 1965, the same specific unemployment rates would have yielded a national rate about 0.2 per cent higher. [See Gertrude Bancroft in R. A. Gordon and M. S. Gordon (eds.), *Prosperity and Unemployment* (New York: John Wiley and Sons, 1966), p. 209. She compares 1957 and 1964.] The Council of Economic Advisers estimated this difference at 0.1 per cent (comparing 1965 and March 1957). (*Economic Report of the President*, January 1966, p. 75.) Lester Thurow estimates

a rise of 0.5–0.6 per cent in frictional unemployment between 1953 and 1966. (Part of this we would call a rise in structural unemployment.) See his paper in R. A. Gordon (ed.), *Toward a Manpower Policy* (New York: John Wiley and Sons, 1967). It should be mentioned that the detailed figures for 1966, during which the unemployment rate averaged less than 4 per cent, were not available when this manuscript was sent to the press. Also, as noted in the Preface, several definitional changes were made in the unemployment data beginning in 1967, and the BLS has revised some previous years' figures to reflect one of these changes, the omission of 14- and 15-year-olds. All data in this chapter are before this revision; i.e., they include 14- and 15-year-olds unless otherwise specified.

2. It can be safely assumed that this rise in D_u in the 1960's would have been even more pronounced had our dispersion measure reflected the differential incidence of disguised as well as of recorded unemployment.

3. 3.8 per cent compared to 0.2 per cent. See *Manpower Report of the President,* March 1966, Statistical Appendix, p. 162.

4. See the papers by Margaret S. Gordon and Gertrude Bancroft in Gordon and Gordon (eds.), *op. cit.*

5. It should be noted, however, that labor force participation rates have declined during the last decade for men in this age group. The decline has been modest for men aged 45–54: from 96.6 per cent in 1956 to 95.6 per cent in 1965. For men 55–64, the decline has been more pronounced: from 88.5 per cent in 1956 to 84.7 per cent in 1965. These trends have not been reversed by the sharp drop in the unemployment rate for each of these groups during 1961–1965. For the 45–54 group, the participation rate was the same in 1965 and 1961; for the 55–64 group, the decline in labor force participation *accelerated* after 1961. (See *Manpower Report of the President,* March 1966, Statistical Appendix, p. 154.) (The spread of more generous provisions for early retirement is undoubtedly a factor here.) It would appear that labor force participation for males 45–64 is not particularly sensitive to changes in employment—much less so than that of males under 25 or 65 and over or that of women. See, for example, Thomas Dernburg and Kenneth Strand, "Hidden Unemployment 1953–62: A Quantitative Analysis by Age and Sex," *American Economic Review,* LVI (March 1966), 71–95; also Jacob Mincer, "Labor Force Participation and Unemployment: A Review of Recent Evidence," in Gordon and Gordon (eds.), *op cit.,* especially pp. 86–88. Mincer cites a number of other studies that have sought to measure the sensitivity of labor force participation, by age and sex, to changing employment conditions.

6. The relative u_i/u for males aged 20–24 was as low as 1.18 in 1951, but in no other postwar year did it fall below 1.48, until it declined to 1.37 in 1965.

7. This statement may need some but not much modification to allow for a possible increase in disguised unemployment among teen-agers during the 1950's. If we raise all age-sex unemployment rates by Dernburg and Strand's estimates of disguised unemployment, the adjusted u_i/u for male

teen-agers *fell* slightly between 1953 and 1959, while the adjusted rates for female teen-agers rose from 2.45 to 3.13. Compare Dernburg and Strand, *op. cit.*, especially p. 90.

8. We must be careful here if we are interested in precise timing. Unemployment rates for teen-agers have a smaller relative amplitude over the cycle than does the national unemployment rate. Hence both of our measures for teen-agers, u_i/u and $(U_i/U - L_i/L)$, will appear to worsen when employment conditions improve, as they did after 1961. (See the discussion of the cyclical behavior of our relative dispersion measure for the age-sex classification in Chapter 5.) For male teen-agers there was a particularly sharp increase in both u_i/u and $(U_i/U - L_i/L)$ between 1962 and 1963, although u did not fall at all; in 1963 both u_i/u and $(U_i/U - L_i/L)$ were considerably higher for both male and female teen-agers than they were in 1960, although the national unemployment rate was almost the same in both years.

9. Since labor force participation rates for teen-agers are sensitive to changing employment opportunities, it may be assumed that disguised unemployment among teen-agers was also higher in 1965 than in the mid-fifties. Figures for 1966 that became available after this monograph had been sent to the press indicate that the *relative* position of teen-agers (as measured by u_i/u) did not improve in 1966. Indeed, the relative position of girls worsened further.

10. The teen-age proportion of the labor force is not expected to rise further until 1975, and should fall back to about 9.4 per cent by 1980. See *Manpower Report of the President,* March 1966, Statistical Appendix, p. 215.

11. The situation of the 16–17 year olds is worse than these figures imply because of increasing disguised unemployment among school dropouts. There has been a marked decline in labor force participation rates among 14–17 year olds not in school. See W. C. Bowen and F. H. Harbison (eds.), *Unemployment in a Prosperous Economy* (Princeton: Princeton University Press, 1965), pp. 33, 35.

12. For a detailed survey of the labor-market status of 16–21-year-olds no longer in school, as of 1963, see Vera C. Perrella, F. A. Bogan, and Thomas E. Swanstrom, *Out-of-School Youth, February 1963,* Bureau of Labor Statistics, Special Labor Force Reports Nos. 46–47 (1964).

13. Nonwhites may be at a disadvantage in the labor market either because of discrimination in hiring, given their skills and other relevant characteristics (other than color), or because the environment makes it difficult for them to acquire the same education, skills, and other relevant attributes as whites. For an interesting attempt to separate the effects of these two sets of influences, see H. J. Gilman, "Economic Discrimination and Unemployment," *American Economic Review,* LV (December 1965), 1077–1096.

14. Based on annual data not shown here.

15. If we look at the annual figures, whatever improvement there has been has occurred only since 1962. For the situation up to 1962, see

also M. A. Kessler, *Economic Status of Nonwhite Workers, 1955–62,* Bureau of Labor Statistics, Special Labor Force Report No. 33 (1963). As this was being prepared for the press, the Bureau of Labor Statistics reported some relative deterioration in the position of nonwhites during the spring and summer of 1966. It is too early to evaluate the long-run significance of this development. See *Employment and Earnings and Monthly Report on the Labor Force* (September 1966), and *New York Times,* September 11, 1966. Figures for all of 1966 indicate that for the year as a whole u_i/u for nonwhites was higher than it had been since 1962. This deterioration in 1966 was almost entirely among nonwhite females. u_i/u for nonwhite males rose only very slightly in 1966.

16. Interestingly, if we accept the official figures at their face value, in 1948 nonwhite male teen-ager unemployment rates were closer to those of whites in the same age-sex group than those of nonwhite adults. This difference had largely disappeared by 1959.

17. There was no reduction between 1956 and 1965 in the participation rate for the nonwhite 20–24 group, although that for whites in this group did show some decline. As for teen-agers, the issue is complicated by educational trends involving more schooling. In view of the sharp increase in the unemployment rate for nonwhite teen-agers, particularly when we consider the sensitivity of labor force participation of this group to the level of unemployment, we may assume that there has been a significant increase in disguised unemployment among nonwhites in the 14–19 age group. We have not, however, tried to measure this increase, although it would have been desirable to make an additional allowance for the increase in disguised unemployment among at least 18- and 19-year-olds. With regard to females, except possibly in the teen-age group, the reverse of disguised unemployment is likely to be true. If unemployment conditions deteriorate for males, more nonwhite females enter the labor force as extra workers. At all ages from 20 up, female participation rates are higher for nonwhites than for whites.

18. As Walter Heller has put it: "If a substantial part of the increase in unemployment since 1957 were accounted for by this explanation, one would expect to find unusually large increases in unemployment (*a*) among blue-collar workers whose former jobs were vulnerable to displacement by automation, and (*b*) among goods-producing industries—mining, manufacturing, construction, transportation, and public utilities—which have so far experienced the most extensive automation." From his paper in A. M. Ross (ed.), *Unemployment and the American Economy* (New York: John Wiley and Sons, 1964), p. 97.

19. As this was being prepared for the press, the Bureau of Labor Statistics reported that there had apparently been some relative deterioration in the position of unskilled laborers and semiskilled operatives in the summer of 1966 (comparing May–August 1966 with January–April 1966, on a seasonally adjusted basis). *Employment and Earnings and Monthly Reports on the Labor Force* (September 1966). Complete annual figures for 1966, however, revealed no relative deterioration for semiskilled operatives and only nominal deterioration for unskilled laborers.

20. The farm laborers' fraction of total unemployment reached a postwar low of 2.6 per cent in 1962, rose to 3.4 per cent in 1964, and decreased to 3.0 per cent in 1965.

21. The sharp drop in the relative importance of first job seekers in 1953 was associated with a decline in the overall unemployment rate to the lowest level reached in the postwar period. My best guess is that this very low level of unemployment among first job seekers in 1953, if not a statistical aberration, reflected the culmination of the very tight labor market during the Korean period. The national unemployment rate not only reached its lowest level of the postwar period in 1953, but was nearly as low in 1951 and 1952. The unemployment rate nearly doubled between 1953 and 1954. In 1953 it was abnormally easy for initial job seekers to find employment, and to find it quickly. It is also worth noting in this connection, that the proportion of the unemployment out of work 15 weeks or longer also reached its postwar low in 1953.

22. As William Haber has put it: "The trend of building fences around the jobs for those who have them is bound to increase . . . . When extended to major plants and industries across the land, it 'fences in' those who work and makes more difficult the admission into such plants and industries of new entrants to the labor force." See his paper in Ross (ed.), *op. cit.*, pp. 33–34.

23. "The Composition of Unemployment and Public Policy," in Gordon and Gordon (eds.), *op. cit.*, pp. 227–245.

24. See Gordon and Gordon (eds.), *op. cit., passim.*

25. See particularly three papers by C. C. Killingsworth, one read at a Conference on Employment Security at Michigan State University, October 26, 1963, one reproduced in *Nation's Manpower Revolution,* Hearings before the Subcommittee on Employment and Manpower of the Senate Committee on Labor and Public Welfare, 88th Congress, 1st Session (Washington, D.C.: September–November 1963), Part 5, pp. 1461–1483, and a third in Jack Stieber (ed.), *Employment Problems of Automation and Advanced Technology: An International Perspective* (London: Macmillan, 1966), pp. 128–156.

26. See also D. F. Johnston and H. R. Hamel, "Educational Attainment of Workers in March 1965," *Monthly Labor Review,* **LXXXIX** (March 1966), 250–257.

27. The data on education and unemployment come from special surveys which were not taken every year. Hence the particular selection of years in Table 6.12. Moreover, the surveys began only in 1952; our figures for 1950 are derived from the census for that year.

28. See also Gertrude Bancroft in Gordon and Gordon (eds.), *op. cit.,* p. 215.

29. The relative worsening for women with no more than four years of schooling was concentrated in 1965. There had been some improvement between 1959 and 1964.

30. *Educational Attainment of Workers, March 1965,* Special Labor Force Report No. 65 (Washington: Government Printing Office, 1966), p. A-6. 1965 and 1957 figures are for March; 1952 for October.

31. The figures for $(U_i/U - L_i/L)$ for college graduates in Table 6.13 do not show the worsening described here. This is because u_i/u was less than one, and L_i/L increased relatively more than the absolute value of $(u_i/u - 1)$ declined. See Chapter 5.

32. This point is particularly emphasized by Killingsworth. See his papers previously cited; also his comment in Gordon and Gordon (eds.), *op. cit.*, pp. 249–251. See also W. H. Gruber, *Productivity, Education and Changes in the Labor Force* (unpublished dissertation, Massachusetts Institute of Technology, 1965), in which the relative importance of disguised unemployment among the least educated is also emphasized.

33. See particularly R. J. Flanagan, "Disguised Unemployment and the Structural Hypothesis," *Industrial Relations,* V (October 1965), 25–30; also Johnston and Hamel, *op. cit.*, pp. 255–257.

34. For additional consideration of this topic, see Susan S. Holland, *Long-Term Unemployment in the 1960's.* Bureau of Labor Statistics, Special Labor Force Report No. 58 (1965).

35. For further consideration of the relation between long-term and total unemployment, see N. J. Simler, "Long-Term Unemployment, the Structural Hypothesis, and Public Policy," *American Economic Review,* LIV (December 1964), 985–1001. A postscript might be added here based on the figures for 1966 which became available after this had gone to press. In 1966, long-term unemployment (both 15 weeks or more and 27 weeks or more) had fallen to as low a fraction of total unemployment as in 1956.

36. Based on figures in *Employment and Earnings and Monthly Report on the Labor Force* (February 1966), p. 20. It is also worth noting that while the official unemployment rate for 1965 (4.6 per cent) was somewhat higher than that in 1956 and 1957 (4.2 and 4.3 per cent, respectively), the estimate of total labor time lost was only 5.0 per cent in 1965 compared to 5.1 per cent in 1956 and 5.3 per cent in 1957.

37. See *Manpower Report of the President,* March 1966, p. 178.

38. We have not included in this chapter anything about the *regional* dispersion of unemployment rates. There are two reasons for this omission. First, local and state data on unemployment rates are not very reliable. Second, the available data on unemployment according to labor market areas are seriously incomplete. We did, however, experiment by computing our relative dispersion index for the following two groups of major local labor areas: 107 areas with complete annual data from 1957 through 1964 and 145 areas (including the 107) with annual data since 1960. For the first group, D_u fell sharply between 1957–1958 and 1960, declined moderately further until 1963, and rose in 1964. For the larger group of 145 areas, D_u showed a significant net increase between 1960 and 1964. I should judge, however, that were the data for all of the 145 areas available for the mid-1950's, D_u for this larger sample would have shown some net decrease between, say, 1957 and 1964. (Data for 1965 became available only after these calculations were made.) It would seem, therefore, that the changing regional pattern of unemployment does not

require any significant modification in the conclusions reached in this and the following paragraphs.

39. A third change, which has been occurring all through the postwar period, should also be mentioned here, although the results of this change on the pattern of unemployment do not appear clearly in the figures that we have presented. This is the heavy migration from farm to city, particularly of poorly educated workers, both white and nonwhite. While the rapid increase in the nonwhite population in the metropolitan centers in the North, Midwest, and California helps to explain the high rates of Negro unemployment in these centers, the result has not been, during the last decade, to raise the nonwhite share of total unemployment nationally or to raise the national unemployment rate for nonwhites relative to the overall rate (see Table 6.5).

40. *Manpower Report of the President,* March 1966, p. 180.

41. These comparisons are based on figures in *Economic Report of the President,* January 1966, p. 235. It should be noted that this particular relationship between u_i and u has a strong cyclical pattern. The rate for married men rises relative to the total rate when the latter increases, and falls when overall unemployment declines.

42. See the labor force projections in *Manpower Report of the President,* March 1966, p. 216.

CHAPTER 7

Toward Full Employment

This monograph is part of a large-scale study of Unemployment and the American Economy which had its inception in the summer of 1962. At that time the unemployment rate was above 5.5 per cent, and 1962 was to mark the fifth consecutive year that the annual average unemployment rate remained above this figure. Indeed the annual figure did not fall below 5 per cent until 1965.

In 1962 a troubled debate was going on regarding the reasons for the persistently high level of unemployment in the United States. Although a new Administration, dedicated to the goal of full employment, had moved into the White House in 1961, there was yet no indication that public opinion was sufficiently aroused to push Congress into taking strong fiscal action to raise aggregate demand and thereby reduce the level of unemployment. Concern was growing, however, regarding the very high unemployment rates in particular regions and among some sectors of the population, and this concern was strengthened by vague but growing fears regarding the impact of technological change and of a changing pattern of demand on the employability of the less skilled and less educated parts of the labor force. As a result, beginning with the Area Redevelopment Act in 1961 and the Manpower Development and Training Act in 1962, the federal government began to develop a manpower program to increase the employability of some of the unemployed. However, these first steps toward dealing with problems of structural unemployment were taken in an environment which was not very sympathetic to risking an increase in the federal deficit and possible further deterioration in the balance of payments in order to bring down the overall unemployment rate to 4 per cent or less.

In the summer of 1962, as we sought to peer ahead, it was easy to take a pessimistic view about how soon unemployment in the United States would again fall to 4 per cent or below. Prevailing attitudes in and out of Congress (although not in the White House or the Council of Economic Advisers) suggested a social welfare function in which welfare was being maximized with an unemployment rate well above 4 per cent, an underlying rate of growth in GNP of perhaps 3 to 3.5 per cent, the best record regarding price stability of any of the advanced industrial countries, and some slow improvement in the balance of payments.

Changes Since 1962

The prospects for achieving and maintaining a reasonably high standard of full employment in the United States have altered significantly in the last few years. A number of factors have occurred to bring about this change.

Clearer understanding. First, there is now a clearer understanding of the factors responsible for the high level of unemployment in the United States in the seven or eight years after 1957.[1] The chief factor was clearly the failure of aggregate demand to rise rapidly enough. There is now fairly general agreement that automation and the changing structure of demand were not major forces keeping unemployment at a high level. At the same time, there has come to be, even among those emphasizing the deficiency-of-demand explanation, a clearer understanding of the role which structural factors have played in determining the level and composition of unemployment in the United States in the postwar years. First, there is a growing appreciation of the heterogeneous character of the American labor force and of the fact that we now have, and always have had, structural imbalances between demand and supply for particular kinds of labor. This, of course, is not a new development. In addition, however, some structural changes have been occurring, particularly on the *supply* side of the labor market. These changes have been of several kinds. First, as we saw in Chapter 6, there is the sharp increase in the supply of teen-agers entering the labor market. Taken in conjunction with the trend toward greater job security for experienced workers, this has led to a marked increase in the share of total unemployment made up of young people seeking their first job. Second, the share of the labor force composed of women has continued to increase. And third, the sharp decline in agricultural employment has accelerated migration from farm to city and the resulting augmentation of the urban labor supply. This has been particularly true of the nonwhite labor force, and to some degree underemployment on the farm has become recorded unemployment in the city. (Nonetheless, this has not led to a rise in the ratio of the nonwhite to the white unemployment rate for the nation as a whole over the last decade.)

Changes in the welfare function. Some significant changes in the nature of the welfare function guiding economic policy in the United States have occurred in the 1960's. In Chapter 2, we related welfare (as viewed by the policy-maker) to the level of unemployment, the rate of change in the price level, and the rate of growth in total output, subject to a series of constraints of which the primary one was balance-of-payments equilibrium. Moreover, we suggested that in the United States we should probably also include in the welfare function some fiscal variable such as the budgetary surplus or deficit of the federal government or the rate of increase in federal nondefense spending.

The evolution of economic policy in the United States since 1961 suggests that the following changes have occurred in the implicit welfare function governing Congressional attitudes toward the goal of full employment. (With respect to each of the changes to be mentioned, it is probably fair to say that Congress has lagged behind the Administration.)

1. Greater importance is now attached to the rate of economic growth.[2] The example not only of Russia but also of the Western European countries and Japan has led to a stronger desire, both in and out of Washington, for a more rapid rate of growth in

real GNP. At the same time the Council of Economic Advisers has widely disseminated the notion of potential GNP and has stressed the need to increase total spending on goods and services as rapidly as potential GNP expands in response to rising productivity and growth of the labor force. Thus the desire for rapid economic growth more strongly reinforces the desire for lower unemployment today than at the end of the 1950's. The result is a greater willingness, in and out of Congress, to undertake expansionary measures that will have this combined effect.[3]

2. The success of the tax cut in 1964 seems to have effected a significant change in the way the fiscal variables enter into the welfare function. To state that Congress and the American public are coming to accept the New (or Keynesian) Economics is to state, at least in part, that a given rise in the federal deficit or in the size of the federal debt outstanding is considered to reduce welfare less today than would have been the general view at the beginning of the 1960's. There is also greater recognition of the fact that if a tax reduction does stimulate spending, total tax revenues may actually increase. Congress and the more informed public have learned about the "full employment surplus," that is, the budgetary surplus that would exist, with given tax rates and spending programs, if total income and output were at the full employment level.

In brief, greater sophistication in matters of fiscal policy has led Congress and the public to be more willing to use fiscal measures to reduce unemployment today than when the Kennedy Administration came into office in 1961.

3. There has been growing public concern over the relatively heavy incidence of unemployment in certain segments of the labor force. In effect, specific unemployment rates for particular groups, as well as the national unemployment rate, now enter importantly into the welfare function. In terms of the welfare function described in Chapter 2, we might say that there has been a change from

$$Z = f(u, \dot{P}, \dot{Y})$$

to

$$Z = f(u, u_1, u_2 \ldots u_i, \dot{P}, \dot{Y})$$

where $u_1, u_2 \ldots u_i$ are the unemployment rates for those groups in the population with the most serious unemployment problems. Emphasis is being placed particularly on the unemployment problems of youth and Negroes, but attention has also been directed to the relatively heavy unemployment among the unskilled, the least educated, and the populations of depressed areas.

This greatly increased concern with the unemployment problems of particular groups has led to the development of a federal manpower program.[4] This program can be said to have begun with the Area Redevelopment Act (1961),[5] which was followed by the Manpower Development and Training Act (1962), the Vocational Education Act (1963), the Education Acts of 1964 and 1965, legislation (in 1964) and administrative action to prevent discrimination in employment, and the Economic Opportunity Act of 1964 (setting up the antipoverty program). In effect, we have introduced specific unemployment rates into our welfare function and at the same time developed some new policy instruments, in the form of various manpower and related programs, to help bring about declines in these relatively high unemployment rates.

We have already noted that these pieces of manpower legislation represented an attack on the "structural" aspects of unemployment. Furthermore, the earlier pieces of this legislation, in 1961–1963, reflected a concern with the *pattern* of unemployment before the necessary steps had been taken, primarily through fiscal action, to bring down the *overall level* of unemployment. It is clear, also, that the action taken to reduce particular unemployment rates (from MDTA to the various pieces of the Poverty Program) was in response to a much broader social welfare function than the one with which we have been concerned. The reduction of particular groups' unemployment rates becanᵉ one of the means of working toward certain broad social goals, such as improving the social and political as well as economic position of the Negro, removing the social tensions resulting from youth unemployment, improving the opportunities for self-improvement among the most disadvantaged, and so on. Or to restate the same point a bit differently, there has developed increased awareness of and sensitivity to the broad social costs and political strains that are associated with high unemployment among some parts of the labor force, even though for the nation as a whole unemployment does not seem high in the light of past experience.[6]

4. As unemployment fell during 1965 and 1966, as job shortages began to develop in some occupations and in some parts of the country, and as worries regarding inflation spread and deepened, another aspect of manpower and employment policy came to be emphasized. There was an increasing recognition that an effective manpower program (including counseling, training and retraining, redesigning jobs, and more effective placement) could help to meet partial labor shortages, reduce frictional unemployment, and simultaneously reduce the number of both job vacancies and persons unemployed.[7] In short, manpower policy could move the Phillips curve and the vacancies-unemployment curve to the left (see Figs. 4.3 and 4.4), thereby reducing the degree of wage and price inflation corresponding to any level of unemployment and increasing the potential level of output for a labor force of a given size. The result, also, is to give us a lower overall level of unemployment corresponding to the goal of full employment.

To summarize briefly: The United States was taking the goal of full employment considerably more seriously by 1966 than five or six years earlier. While the balance-of-payments constraint was still powerful, and while a considerable value was still put on price stability for its own sake, the fear of government deficits had diminished and a new importance was being placed on the need to reduce the differentially high unemployment among the disadvantaged parts of the labor force. The United States was beginning to move toward a policy of *structural* as well as *aggregative* full employment. And the balancing of various economic and social objectives that reflected a changing public consensus was leading toward a higher standard for the goal of aggregative full employment than had existed during the first decade and a half after World War II.

Disaggregating the Full Employment Goal

What is a reasonable full employment goal for the United States to strive for during the decade ahead? We have already suggested that the goal should be defined in structural as well as aggregative terms. To recapitulate, it is not enough to ask what overall unemployment rate we arrive at when, in terms of some welfare function, we weigh the gains from reducing unemployment by various amounts against the associated costs, particularly the cost in an accelerated rise in prices. To do no more than this is to take the existing amount and distribution of frictional and structural unemployment as given.

Let us ask, therefore, what pattern of unemployment rates—by age, sex, color, and occupation—can we hope to achieve by appropriate manpower and other policies? Unfortunately, there is no existing evidence permitting us to establish functional relationships that would describe how specific unemployment rates might decline in response to increasing government expenditures on various types of manpower and related programs. Hence we are in no position to reach a conclusion about an optimal pattern of unemployment rates, given our particular evaluation of the costs and benefits involved. Even so, it may be useful to offer some conjectures on how far we might be able to reduce particular unemployment rates, especially those that are relatively high, and to ask what overall unemployment rate would result from such a new pattern of unemployment rates by, for example, age, sex, and color.

Age and sex. Let us begin with the age-sex classification of the labor force. The first three columns of Table 7.1 present the unemployment rates for the various age-sex groups that were actually experienced in 1953, 1956, and 1965—years in which the overall unemployment rates were, respectively, 2.9, 4.2, and 4.6 per cent. Column 4 of the table offers a set of guesses as to how low we might be able to bring the various age-sex unemployment rates by appropriate policies without radical change in the existing institutional framework.

In arriving at these hypothetical rates, I started with the rates for males aged 25–44 and 45–64. Here I took the rates which existed in 1953, rates which were approximately duplicated in the first half of 1966. Quite arbitrarily, I assumed unemployment rates of 4 per cent for males 20–24 and 6 per cent for male teen-agers, rates which are, respectively, slightly less than two and three times the rate for men in the prime working-age

TABLE 7.1.   Unemployment by Age and Sex: Hypothetical Full Employment Target Compared
With Actual Data for 1953, 1956, and 1965 (Per Cent)

Age and Sex	Unemployment Rate			Target Unemployment Rate	Contribution to Overall Rate (1965 Weights)
	1953	1956	1965		
Males	2.8	3.8	4.0		1.80
14–19	7.3	10.2	13.1	6.0	.33
20–24	5.0	6.9	6.3	4.0	.26
25–44	2.1	2.9	2.7	2.1	.58
45–64	2.5	3.2	2.8	2.5	.56
65 and over	2.4	3.5	3.5	2.5	.07
Females	3.3	4.9	5.5		1.17
14–19	6.8	10.8	14.3	6.0	.23
20–24	4.3	6.3	7.3	4.3	.19
25–44	2.9	4.3	5.0	3.2	.43
45–64	2.4	3.6	3.1	2.4	.30
65 and over	1.4	2.3	2.8	2.0	.03
Total	2.9	4.2	4.6		2.97

Source: Actual data are from Manpower Report of the President, March 1966, Statistical
Appendix.   For the basis of the target unemployment rates, see the explanation to the text.

group. These rates are lower than those achieved even in 1953.
Compared to the situation in mid-1966 (not shown in the table),
only a moderate further decline would be required for the 20–24
group, but our 6 per cent rate for male teen-agers is only about
half the rate (seasonally adjusted) in mid-1966. For males 65
and over, I have assumed a rate slightly higher than in 1953.

For women, I considered some of the differential trends in
labor force participation and unemployment described in Chapter 6. For the female 25–44 group, I increased the 1953 rate
by 10 per cent; I adopted the 1953 rates for the 20–24 and
45–64 age groups; and I raised the 1953 figure for the 65 and
over group. For teen-age girls, I took the same 6 per cent figure
used for boys.

Two assumptions underlying the figures chosen should be noted
particularly. One is that minimum frictional unemployment for
males in the prime working-age group probably cannot be pushed
down much below 2 per cent.[8] The second is that, at not unrea-

sonable cost, unemployment among teen-agers can be brought
down to 6 per cent.

Now examine the last column of Table 7.1. If we weight our
age-specific unemployment targets by each group's share of the
labor force in 1965, the overall unemployment rate turns out
to be almost exactly 3 per cent. If we were to substitute the
age-sex distribution projected for 1975 (not shown in Table 7.1),
the overall rate would remain at approximately 3 per cent. Here,
then, is one pattern of age-sex unemployment rates that yields
the frequently cited figure of 3 per cent as the target for full
employment.

No strong argument can be made for this particular set of
unemployment rates, and we cannot offer a detailed program,
with an estimate of the costs involved, that would, with a high
degree of probability, yield this pattern of unemployment rates
within a specified time. Nonetheless the exercise does serve a
useful purpose. It warns us that an overall unemployment rate
of 3 or 3.5 per cent can be associated with a number of different
patterns of rates by age and sex; it reminds us that a very
large decline in, say, the male teen-age unemployment rate may
have only a moderate effect on the overall rate; we begin to
have a rough notion of the limit below which we are not likely
to be able to drive the lowest rates; and, in general, we are
made more sensitive to the character and magnitude of the structural problems involved in achieving and maintaining an overall
rate of as low as, for example, 3 per cent.

Color. Let us now introduce the additional element of color
into our examination of possible target unemployment rates. In
recent years, the nonwhite unemployment rate has remained at
about twice that for whites. By how much can we hope to reduce
this differential? In 1953, with an overall unemployment rate
of 2.9 per cent, the rate for nonwhites was still two-thirds higher
than that for whites.

In Table 7.2 I have taken as a goal a nonwhite unemployment
rate that is only one-third higher than that for whites and assumed that this differential would hold for all age-sex groups.
This differential, applied to the combined white-nonwhite rates
by age and sex in Table 7.1, yields the target unemployment
rates in Table 7.2. (In the second table we show only two age

TABLE 7.2. Unemployment by Color, Sex, and Age: Hypothetical Full Employment Target
Compared with Actual Data for 1953, 1956, and 1965 (Per Cent)

Color, Sex, and Age	Unemployment Rate			Target Unemployment Rate	Contribution to Overall Rate (1965 Weights)
	1953	1956	1965		
White	2.7	3.7	4.1	2.9	2.58
Both sexes, 14–19	7.0	9.5	12.2	5.8	.49
Males, 20 and over	2.3	3.0	2.9	2.4	1.28
Females, 20 and over	2.7	3.7	4.0	3.0	.81
Nonwhite	4.5	8.4	8.3	3.9	.44
Both sexes, 14–19	7.9	17.4	25.3	7.7	.08
Males, 20 and over	4.5	7.3	6.0	3.2	.19
Females, 20 and over	3.7	7.8	7.4	4.0	.17
Total	2.9	4.2	4.6		3.02

Source: The actual data are from Manpower Report of the President, March 1966, Statistical
Appendix. For the basis of the target unemployment rates, see the explanation in the text.

groups, 14–19 and 20 and over.) When the individual rates are
appropriately weighted, we get unemployment rates of 2.9 for
whites, 3.9 for nonwhites, and 3.0 per cent overall. The nonwhite
rate of 3.9 per cent compares with that of 4.5 per cent achieved
in 1953.

Given the growing efforts being invested in improving the employability of Negroes and assuming a continued high level of
aggregate demand, can we hope to bring the nonwhite unemployment rate down to around 4 per cent? Obviously, it will be
very difficult to achieve this goal during the next decade.[9]

With nonwhites making up only about 11 per cent of the
labor force, large changes in the nonwhite rate have only a small
effect on the overall rate of unemployment. Thus, if the rates
for whites remained as they are in Table 7.2, a 6 per cent rate
for nonwhites instead of our assumed 4 per cent would raise
the overall rate from 3.0 to only 3.2 per cent. This merely elabo-
rates an obvious point. The urgent sense of need now prevailing
in the United States to reduce the nonwhite unemployment rate
centers on the direct benefits of this improvement for the Negro
population—and indirectly on the benefit for the entire population achieved through the reduction of political and social ten-

TABLE 7.3.   Unemployment by Occupation: Hypothetical Full Employment Target Compared with Actual Data for 1953, 1957, and 1965 (Per Cent)

Occupation	Unemployment Rate			Target Unemployment Rate	Contribution to Overall Rate (1965 Weights)
	1953	1957	1965		
White-collar	1.4	2.0	2.3	1.7	0.73
Professional, technical	0.9	1.2	1.5	1.0	0.12
Managers, officials, proprietors	0.9	1.0	1.1	1.0	0.10
Clerical	1.7	2.8	3.2	2.3	0.35
Sales	2.1	2.6	3.3	2.5	0.16
Blue-collar	3.5	6.1	5.3	3.6	1.32
Craftsmen, foremen	2.6	3.8	3.6	2.6	0.33
Operatives	3.2	6.3	5.5	3.8	0.71
Laborers	6.1	9.4	8.4	5.0	0.28
Service	3.2	4.8	5.2	3.6	0.47
Household workers	2.5	3.7	4.2	2.5	0.08
Others	3.6	5.1	5.5	4.0	0.40
Farm	1.1	1.9	2.6	1.7	0.10
Farmers and farm managers	0.2	0.3	0.4	0.3	0.01
Farm laborers and foremen	2.5	3.7	4.8	3.3	0.09
No previous work experience	---				0.36
Total	2.5	4.3	4.6		2.98

Source: Actual data are from Manpower Report of the President, March 1966, Statistical Appendix. For the basis of the target unemployment rates, see the explanation in the text.   Data for 1953 have not been revised to correspond to the definitions used in 1957 and later years.

sions that would result from a marked decline in the nonwhite unemployment rate.[10]

Occupation. Let us continue with this speculative exercise and set some unemployment targets by occupation that are consistent with those that we have suggested for the various age, sex, and color groups. This we do in Table 7.3, which is comparable with Tables 7.1 and 7.2 in all but one respect. The occupational data on unemployment for 1956 and earlier are not fully comparable with those for later years. A change in definitions in 1957 resulted in moderately raising the overall unemployment rate. While the official figures for the age, sex, and color classifications for the earlier years have been revised, this is not true for the occupational breakdown.

Thus the figures for 1953 in Table 7.3 yield an overall unemployment rate of 2.5 per cent, whereas on the basis of the definitions underlying the 1957 and 1965 figures the national rate would have been 2.9 per cent. The occupational unemployment rates for 1953 therefore must be raised somewhat—on the average by roughly one-sixth (but not necessarily in the same proportion for each occupation).

In setting our hypothetical targets, we have again been guided by what was achieved in 1953 (with a rough allowance for the necessary upward adjustment just described). In all cases, the targets are below the lowest quarterly rate achieved in the first half of 1966, when the national unemployment rate averaged 3.85 per cent. The sharpest contrast is in the case of laborers, where our target of 5 per cent compares with a rate probably close to 7 per cent (after appropriate adjustment) in 1953 and more than 7 per cent in 1966.

In Chapter 6, in discussing trends in the occupational pattern of unemployment, we noted the fact that the proportion of the unemployed represented by those without previous work experience had been increasing for more than a decade (see Table 6.9). In 1953 the inexperienced made up only 4.4 per cent of the unemployed;[11] in 1965 the figure was 17.7 per cent. In Table 7.3 we have reduced this to 12 per cent to reflect the amount by which we have reduced the teen-age unemployment rate in Table 7.1. With the accelerated influx of teen-agers into the labor force in recent years, we must assume that for a considerable time to come the inexperienced will constitute a larger fraction of total unemployment than they did in the early or middle 1950's.

Again, since essentially the same standards were used as in the preceding examples, our structural targets yield an overall unemployment rate of just about 3 per cent. To push the national rate much lower than this, with no change in the occupational pattern of the labor force, we should have to set still lower target rates particularly for those groups making the largest contributions to total unemployment: clerical workers, blue-collar workers (particularly semiskilled operatives), service workers, and those without previous work experience. We should note, however, that the steady movement from blue-collar to white-collar jobs implies a shift in weighting toward occupations with relatively low unemployment rates. Thus if we apply the target unemployment rates in Table 7.3 to the occupational pattern of the labor force projected for 1975, we get an overall unemployment rate of 2.9 rather than 3.0 per cent.

Another approach. Another way of approaching the problem of reducing unemployment among specific groups is to estimate the unemployment-reducing effects of various combinations of manpower programs of the sort that are already in existence. An example of this approach was recently presented by Philip Arnow of the United States Department of Labor.[12] He suggested a set of programs (directed toward youth, nonwhite adults, the long-term unemployed, and whites in the 20–24 age group) which was "calculated to bring the volume of unemployment down by at least a million, on the basis of current experience and knowledge . . ." within a period of two years, starting with the pattern of unemployment rates that has recently been associated with an overall unemployment rate of 4 per cent. Had such an expanded manpower program been put into effect at the beginning of 1966 and had it achieved the hoped-for results, the national unemployment rate at the beginning of 1968 would presumably be even lower than the 3 per cent that resulted from our sets of targets in Tables 7.1–7.3.[13]

The Aggregative Approach to the Goal of Full Employment

Most of the discussion in recent years regarding an appropriate full employment goal has been expressed in purely aggregative terms, with the amount and pattern of frictional and structural unemployment taken as given. Essentially two sets of issues are involved when the question is stated in these terms.

First, what are the *facts* regarding the relationships that exist among the important variables that enter into the relevant social welfare function? Above all, what is the nature of the critical relation or trade-off that is presumed to hold between the rate of change in prices and the overall level of unemployment? How much of a cost in terms of a rise in the price level must we expect to pay to reduce unemployment by varying amounts?

Second, what are assumed to be the effects on social welfare, as viewed by the parties concerned, of various combinations of the variables that enter into the welfare function? In particular, what are our views as to the welfare implications of alternative combinations of higher or lower unemployment and lower or higher rates of increase in the price level?

The Trade-Off Between Full Employment and Inflation

While numerous attempts have been made to determine the precise relationship between changes in wages and prices, on the one hand, and the level of unemployment, on the other, it cannot be said that our knowledge in this area has yet progressed very far.[14] Although our knowledge is limited, at least the following statements can be made with reasonable safety.

1. There is certainly some rough inverse relation between unemployment and the rate of change in wages, although wage behavior is also affected by other variables in addition to the level of unemployment. The lower the unemployment level (and probably also the faster unemployment is falling), the more rapidly, other things given, will wages tend to rise. We can be fairly confident, also, that this relationship is not an invariant one. It will tend to vary to some extent both in the short run and in the long run.

2. The impact of lower unemployment on wages is likely to be greater the higher the level of profits (and also perhaps the more rapid the rate at which profits are rising).[15] A period of continued low unemployment is likely to be a period of high profits, and thus there may be two (related) sources of upward pressure on wages.[16]

3. The extent to which wage increases are translated into price increases depends primarily on (1) how fast labor productivity is increasing and (2) the behavior of profit margins.[17] The famous wage-price guideposts of the Kennedy and Johnson Administrations were geared to an assumed (trend) rate of increase in national output per man-hour of about 3.2 per cent per year. With no change in average profit margins, wages could presumably rise by this amount without bringing about an upward trend in the price level appropriately defined.

4. The postwar record clearly indicates that, without significant changes in the social and economic environment, we cannot expect to keep the unemployment rate at or below 4 per cent and at the same time avoid an upward trend in the price level— as measured, for example, by the Consumer Price Index or the implicit price deflator for the GNP. As a matter of fact, we have not been able to escape some rise in the price level, as officially measured, even with unemployment rates well above 4 per cent. Between 1957 and 1965, the Consumer Price Index (CPI) rose gradually at an average rate of 1.4 per cent per year. The unemployment rate was 4.3 per cent in 1957, 4.6 per cent in 1965, and more than 5 per cent in all of the intervening years. The rise in prices accelerated as the unemployment rate fell to 4 per cent and less in 1966.[18] It is obvious that an increase in the CPI at the rate of about 1.5 per cent per year has not been considered to involve any significant loss of welfare, particularly when prices were rising more rapidly in most other advanced countries. It was also clear, as the price rise accelerated in 1966, that price increases of the order of 3.0 to 3.5 per cent per year were viewed with considerable alarm—by the Administration, Congress, and the public at large. However, even at this higher rate of inflation, there seemed to be little disposition in Washington to risk a return to unemployment rates much above 4 per cent in order to bring the rise in the CPI back down to a rate of 2 per cent or less.

One opinion expressed at the beginning of the 1960's was that complete price stability in the United States would have required an unemployment rate of between 5 and 6 per cent and that an unemployment rate of 3 per cent would lead to a rise in prices of 4 to 5 per cent a year.[19] A number of formal studies of the wage–unemployment relation in the United States have been made since then. While they all confirm the inverse relation between wage changes and the level of unemployment, they offer different answers as to what other variables are also involved, and they yield different predictions as to how rapidly wages would rise if unemployment were as low as, say, 3 per cent. Tests made on a number of these studies suggest that, at a 3 per cent level of unemployment, wages in manufacturing or in the private economy as a whole would possibly rise at a rate of between 5.5 and perhaps 8 per cent a year. With productivity rising at 3 to 3.5 per cent a year, this implies a rise in the price level of from 2 to 5 per cent a year, depending on the particular relationship we use and what else we take as given. In a recent study, for example, G. L. Perry estimated that, with productivity increasing at 3 per cent and with profits at their average rate during 1953–1960, unemployment of 3 per cent would result in a rise in prices of 3.5 per cent per annum. Under the same assumptions, unemployment of 4 per cent would be associated with an increase in prices of only 1.5 per cent per year.[20]

In general, the lower the rate of profits, the less rapid the rate of decline in unemployment, and the less the recent rise in the Consumer Price Index, the less will be the rise in wages associated with a given level of unemployment. Moreover, given the increase in wages, the rise in prices will be less the more rapid the increase in productivity.

There is general agreement that, given the institutional and structural characteristics of the American economy in the postwar period, unemployment of 4 per cent or less is incompatible with complete price stability. While this conclusion can hardly be challenged, two important points must immediately be noted.

First, we may be willing (indeed, it is clear that we *are* willing) to settle for less than complete price stability. As already mentioned, part of Perry's results just cited suggests that, on one not unreasonable set of assumptions regarding productivity change and profit levels, unemployment of 4 per cent would be compatible with an annual rise in the Consumer Price Index of no more than 1.5 per cent. Most Americans would probably be happy to accept this degree of inflation to keep the unemployment rate no higher than 4 per cent. Moreover, the faster we can increase productivity, the less the degree of inflation associated with any given amount of unemployment.

On the other hand, it may be that most Americans would believe that inflation at the rate of 3.5 per cent a year was too high a price to pay for an unemployment rate of 3 per cent, particularly if 4 per cent unemployment can be purchased at a significantly lower price in terms of inflation.

Now we come to our second point. Full employment and price stability are incompatible, *given the present institutional and structural characteristics of the American economy.* If the institutional and structural environment can be changed, these two goals might become more compatible.

In a sense, the controversial wage-price guideposts of the Kennedy and Johnson Administrations represented an attempt to bring about such institutional changes: to induce organized labor to show restraint in its wage demands as employment opportunities improved and to cajole large-scale business into contenting itself with lower prices than seemed to be called for by the state of the market and prevailing business practice. In the absence of legal compulsion, the guideposts were of limited effectiveness, particularly as aggregate demand rose and unemployment fell.[21] As we saw in Chapter 2, incomes policies are relatively ineffective in restraining wage and price increases under conditions of high employment unless the government is prepared to impose legal restraints on the free operation of labor and commodity markets, for example, as the British Labor Government was finally forced to do in the summer and fall of 1966.[22]

The Importance of Manpower Policy

There is another type of institutional or structural change that does hold out considerable hope for effectuating a better reconciliation between the goals of full employment and price stability.[23] This is through manpower (or labor market) policy, which seeks to bring about a better adjustment of supply to demand in the different parts of the labor market and generally to improve the functioning of the labor market as a whole.[24] That is, manpower policy seeks to reduce the amount of structural and frictional unemployment that exists at aggregative full employment. As we saw in Chapter 4, reducing frictional and structural unemployment causes a shift to the left in the Phillips curve relating unemployment to the rate of change in wages or prices, and permits us to achieve a lower level of total unemployment for any given rate of change in wages or prices. At the same time, a successful manpower policy moves us toward

the goal of "structural full employment," aimed particularly
at improving employment opportunities for the more disadvantaged parts of the labor force.[25]

To put the matter another way, an effective manpower program can reduce the incompatibility between the full employment and price-stability goals in the following ways.

1. Given a heterogeneous labor force, with limited mobility
among sectors and with a considerable degree of downward wage
inflexibility, well designed manpower programs can help to qual-
ify and move unemployed workers in one part of the labor market to another part of the labor market in which there are un-
filled vacancies. This can be done, for example, through improved
education (particularly for underprivileged groups), counseling,
training and retraining (including on-the-job training), provision
of relocation allowances, help to employers in redesigning job
specifications, and in other ways. This is illustrated by Fig.
7.1, which reproduces Fig. 4.5. The broken line *ABCD* shows
the relation between vacancies and unemployment in a labor
market divided into four sectors, representing, for example, four

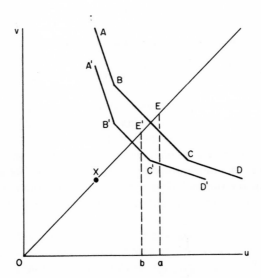

Fig. 7.1. Cross-sectional relation between
vacancies and unemployment.

different levels of skill. There are excess vacancies in sectors
A and B, and unemployment exceeds vacancies in C and D.
If a manpower program qualifies some of the unemployed in
C and D to fill vacancies in A and B, we get the situation
represented by $A'B'C'D'$, and total unemployment declines from
a to b—provided, of course, that aggregate demand rises sufficiently to absorb the additional output. In both situations *total*
vacancies equal *total* unemployment as Figure 7.1 is drawn. (The
figure might be redrawn so that vacancies did not equal unemployment for the economy as a whole. In that case, E and E'
would not fall on the 45-degree line.)

Certainly efforts to achieve an unemployment rate of less than
4 per cent by expanding aggregate demand will entail a smaller
increase in wages and prices if the vacancy–unemployment pattern corresponds to $A'B'C'D'$ than if we have the more unbal-
anced pattern represented by $ABCD$. The movement from
$ABCD$ to $A'B'C'D'$ is equivalent to a shift to the left in the
Phillips curve relating the rate of change in wages to the overall
unemployment rate.[26] Thus far, in the United States our manpower programs have not been on a large enough scale, nor
have they been in effect long enough, to bring about a significant
change of the sort described here.

2. Some types of manpower programs can make a significant
contribution to reducing frictional unemployment. Measures that
reduce the time taken in moving between jobs, that reduce the
time spent by new entrants into the labor force in finding their
first jobs, that even out seasonal changes in unemployment, and,
generally, that improve mobility and the flow of information
in the labor market all serve to reduce frictional unemployment
and, *pari passu*, the amount of unemployment that corresponds
to aggregative full employment.[27] In the United States, a more
effective Federal-State Employment Service should, in particular, be able to bring about a significant decline in frictional
unemployment.[28]

3. Although this is implied in what has already been said,
manpower policy can reduce inflationary pressures at high levels
of employment by preventing (or quickly eliminating) labor
bottlenecks. Part of the upward pressure on wages and prices
in tight labor markets comes from bidding by employers for

skills that are in particularly short supply, and these wage and price increases then spread to other sectors. Improved methods of forecasting manpower demands, effective counseling of prospective entrants into the labor force, improved training and retraining programs, and the redesigning of jobs as needed should minimize the inflationary pressures resulting from efforts to keep unemployment in the United States below, say, the level of 4 per cent.[29]

4. Even under a set of manpower programs more extensive than that now existing in the United States, there will continue to be a hard core of those who are virtually unemployable for various reasons: the physically and mentally handicapped, poorly educated workers who cannot be easily retrained, and others who for one or another reason cannot meet employers' minimal standards. For those unfortunates, unemployment (both open and disguised) can be significantly reduced in only one way, by a program of governmental job creation. Jobs for some of the handicapped can be created in existing government activities, and, in addition, light public works of acknowledged social usefulness can be undertaken for this purpose.[30]

5. Although this carries us considerably beyond the limits of even a broad definition of manpower policy, it is worth making once again the obvious point that part of the problem of structural unemployment in the United States will yield only to far-reaching social and economic reforms, on which the United States has thus far made only a beginning in the anti-poverty program, civil rights legislation, federal aid to education, various housing programs, and other measures to cope with urban blight and rural poverty. Greater equality of opportunity (beginning with the environment in which a child is born and reared and including the education and training which prepare him for adult life) is an essential precondition for the further reduction of poverty and of the hard core of structural unemployment.

Toward a Goal of Three Per Cent

Existing evidence does not permit us to predict with confidence what price in terms of inflation the United States would have to pay for achieving and maintaining any given level of unemployment, whether 4 or 3 or 2 per cent. Nor can this writer predict the nature of the social welfare function that will be reflected in Congress in the years ahead as a result of a political process that mirrors and in some manner blends the conflicting value judgments of the American electorate.

Our informed guess is that, with the help of an expanded and more effective manpower policy (assisted by broader measures to improve the education and environment of the underprivileged), and possibly with some small help from a modified variant of the guideposts, it should be possible to come close to an aggregative full employment goal corresponding to a national unemployment rate of about 3 per cent.[31] This rate could be associated with a pattern of unemployment rates by age, sex, color, and occupation not greatly different from those presented in Tables 7.1–7.3.

The achievement and maintenance of this aggregative and structural full employment goal will involve a cost in terms of an upward secular trend in prices. Certainly, the economies of Western Europe have found it necessary to incur this cost to achieve the relatively high full employment goals that they have maintained in recent years—goals that in general are higher than that which we have suggested for the United States.[32]

The rise in prices that would be associated with the full employment goal that we have suggested would be less the more effective a manpower policy we can develop (along lines that have been suggested here) and the more successful we are in finding an effective way of inducing labor and business to show restraint in their wage demands and price practices.

I should hazard the guess that it should be possible within the next decade to reduce structural and frictional unemployment by an amount equal to 1 per cent of the labor force, so that the inflationary pressures at 3 per cent unemployment would not be much, if any, greater than those that previously existed at 4 per cent. If this result could be achieved—and I do not think that it will be achieved easily or in a year or two—it might be possible to maintain unemployment at 3 per cent with an inflationary price trend of perhaps 1.5–2.5 per cent. The faster the growth in productivity, the more effective are our manpower programs, and the greater the restraint that labor and business can be induced to display, the better are our chances of holding inflation down to the lower end of this range.[33]

As this is being written, the wage-price guideposts are in poor repute, and many assume that this American experiment in incomes policy will soon meet an unhappy end.[34] I suspect, however, that there is room, within the American framework of free labor and commodity markets, for some loose and flexible version of an incomes policy. It would probably be wise not to set fixed guideposts. And certainly, representatives of labor and business should be called in by the Administration for consultation in a more formal and continuous way than now seems to be customary. But, with some imagination, it should be possible to devise a way of continuing to exert a moderate but continuing pressure that would have some modest restraining influence on wages, prices, and profits.[35]

With an expanded and more effective manpower program than we now have, with some modest and flexible variant of an incomes policy, and with some help from a public employment program, the inflationary pressures associated with 3 per cent unemployment should be less than those experienced by most of Western Europe during the last decade. If so, the balance of payments should not prove an insuperable obstacle, although this will depend in good part on the amount of pressure on the dollar resulting from continued large-scale private capital exports and from American aid and military expenditures abroad. Devaluation and a fluctuating exchange rate are alternatives available to overcome the balance-of-payments constraint that official American policy is apparently not yet willing to consider.

A Note of Caution

We have suggested that, with the help of an expanded and more effective manpower program, public employment for the hard-core unemployed, and a modest variant of an incomes policy, the American economy could live with the inflationary pressures associated with unemployment of 3 per cent. But several warnings are in order

1. The more rapidly we move the remaining distance to 3 per cent unemployment, the greater will be the inflationary pressures. There are two reasons for this. First, the rate of increase in wages seems to be associated to some degree with the rate of change in as well as the level of unemployment. Second and more important, the inflationary pressure will be less, as we expand aggregate demand, the more we can reduce structural unemployment, but this takes time.

2. Our setting the full employment goal at an unemployment rate of 3 per cent assumes a larger-scale and more effective manpower program than we now have. It will take time to develop and implement such a program; it will be expensive; and Congress and the American taxpayer may not be willing to incur the expense involved. It is fairly clear that the Clark Subcommittee in 1964 was overly optimistic in its belief that, by an appropriate combination of aggregative and manpower policies, we could reach 3 per cent unemployment by the beginning of 1968 without an unacceptable rise in prices.[36]

3. Continued full employment at a very high level *could* affect the supply curve for labor, shifting it upward, and thus increase the upward pressure on wages. If workers no longer fear unemployment, and the average number of unemployed is significantly reduced, wage increases may turn out to be greater than past experience would suggest. Manpower policy, by reducing structural unemployment, shifts the curve relating wage increases to unemployment to the left. However, the continued maintenance of a very low level of unemployment may cause the curve to shift upward and to the right, so that the same low level of unemployment, if maintained, comes to be associated with larger increases in wages.

In short, striving for an unemployment rate of 3 per cent—and keeping it there—is not without its dangers, and it may well be that Congress and the American public will decide to settle for less. Nevertheless, given the tremendous economic and social benefits to be obtained from placing an additional 750,000 to a million unemployed Americans in productive work, a strong case can be made for trying to push the unemployment rate down toward 3 per cent. We can push in this direction, in the ways suggested, and carefully watch the results. If the rate of price increase begins to become unacceptably large and we are unable to develop (or unwilling to pay for) programs that would hold the degree of inflation within acceptable bounds, we can stop short of a 3 per cent unemployment rate. But all the evidence available suggests that, given prevailing value judgments both in and out of Washington and given what we seem to know about the underlying economic relationships, there is no reason why the United States should settle for an overall unemployment rate higher than 4 per cent.

We feel that the goal should be put closer to 3 than to 4 per cent, although this is an opinion limited both by imperfect knowledge of the underlying relationships and by the configuration of our particular welfare function. In the range of uncertainty between unemployment rates of, say, 3 and 4 per cent, the gains from reducing the unemployment rate seem to be so great that it can reasonably be argued that we should try seriously to move closer to the 3 per cent figure. This is all the more the case if we consider the social, economic, and political gains to be secured from further driving down unemployment among those groups with the highest unemployment rates. If, as we press toward this goal, the inflationary cost turns out to be greater than we are willing to pay, and if we are not prepared to take additional steps (through enlarged manpower programs and in other ways) to damp the rise in wages and prices, we can settle for more than 3 per cent—but hopefully for significantly less than 4 per cent—unemployment. But at least we should *try*.[37] Let us not merely *assume* that the best we can achieve is a national unemployment rate of 4 per cent— and the high rates for nonwhites, youth, and the unskilled that have recently been associated with total unemployment of 4 per cent.[38]

NOTES

1. See R. A. Gordon and M. S. Gordon (eds.), *Prosperity and Unemployment* (New York: John Wiley and Sons, 1966). This paragraph is no more than a summary of pp. 4–5 of that book. See also W. G. Bowen

and F. H. Harbison (eds.), *Unemployment in a Prosperous Economy* (Princeton: Industrial Relations Section, Princeton University, 1965), and A. F. Burns, *The Management of Prosperity* (New York: Columbia University Press, 1966), Lecture 2.

2. As noted in Chapter 2, growth can be stimulated by measures operating to increase aggregate demand and by action to accelerate the growth of aggregate supply (or potential output). Given the growth of the labor force and the trends in labor productivity and in hours worked, we can determine the trend in potential output. If aggregate demand, adjusted for change in the price level, is expanding less rapidly than potential output, unemployment will rise; if demand rises faster than potential output, unemployment will fall until demand equals potential output. Any acceleration in the growth of potential output requires, of course, a corresponding acceleration in the rise in deflated aggregate demand if unemployment is not to increase.

3. At the same time, somewhat greater emphasis is also being placed on stimulating the growth of potential output through measures that accelerate the increase in labor productivity. As we have already noted, acceleration in the growth of potential output requires acceleration in the growth of aggregate demand (in real terms) if unemployment is not to rise. For an interesting account of the new emphasis on growth in American economic policy in the 1960's, see Walter Heller, *New Dimensions of Political Economy* (Cambridge, Mass.: Harvard University Press, 1966), Chap. 2.

4. For a convenient survey of how a manpower program has evolved in the United States, see the paper by Garth Mangum in R. A. Gordon (ed.), *Toward a Manpower Policy* (New York: John Wiley and Sons, 1967). The other papers in this book provide additional background on the development and present status of manpower policy in the United States. See also S. A. Levitan and I. H. Siegel (eds.), *Dimensions of Manpower Policy: Programs and Research* (Baltimore: Johns Hopkins Press, 1966).

5. "At no time prior to 1961 can the United States be said to have had a real manpower policy." Subcommittee on Employment and Manpower of the Senate Committee on Labor and Public Welfare, *Toward Full Employment: Proposals for a Comprehensive Employment and Manpower Policy in the United States*, 88th Congress, 2nd Session (Washington: Government Printing Office, 1964), p. 7. See also pp. 11–12.

6. Compare the evaluation of "The Hidden Costs of Unemployment" by the Secretary of Labor in *Manpower Report of the President,* March 1966, pp. 49 ff.

7. See *Technology and the American Economy,* Report of the National Commission on Technology, Automation, and Economic Progress (Washington: Government Printing Office, 1966), p. 26.

8. The assumed rate of 2.1 per cent for this group covers both whites and nonwhites. In 1966 the ratio of the nonwhite to the white unemployment rate was about two to one. If this differential were maintained,

our assumed rate of 2.1 per cent in Table 7.1 implies an unemployment rate for whites in the 25–44 age group of about 1.9 per cent. If the nonwhite–white ratio were reduced to 1.33 to one, as assumed in Table 7.2, the unemployment rate for white males aged 25–44 implied in Table 7.1 is about 2 per cent.

9. The essential problem here has been well stated by the Commission on Technology, Automation, and Economic Progress: "If trends in upgrading the jobs of nonwhites continue at the same rate as in recent years, the nonwhite unemployment rate in 1975 would still be about 2½ times that for the labor force as a whole. Thus nonwhites must gain access to the rapidly growing higher skilled and white-collar occupations at a faster rate than in the past eight years if their unemployment rate is to be brought down to the common level." *Technology and the American Economy,* p. 31.

10. As this chapter was being completed, the Bureau of Labor Statistics reported that a disconcerting rise in u_i for nonwhites had occurred during the spring and summer of 1966. The ratio of the nonwhite to the national unemployment rate, on a seasonally adjusted basis, averaged 1.98 during May–August 1966, compared to 1.78 during the same period of 1965 and 1.87 during January–April 1966. (See *Employment and Earnings and Monthly Report of the Labor Force,* September 1966.) These ratios compare with 1.80 for all of 1965 and 2.00 in 1956, as shown in our Table 6.5. Later figures indicate that for all of 1966 this ratio turned out to be 1.92, the highest since 1962.

11. As we pointed out in Chapter 6, this percentage was much lower, for 1953 than for the several years preceding or following.

12. Philip Arnow, "What Are Our Manpower Goals?" in R. A. Gordon (ed.), *op. cit.*

13. Probably in the range 2.6–2.8 per cent, the precise figure depending on various assumptions and on whether the million is subtracted from unemployment at the beginning of 1966 or from the amount of unemployment represented by 4 per cent of the larger labor force at the beginning of 1968.

14. A list of the more important studies of the relationship between wage changes and unemployment in the United States is given in Note 18, Chapter 4.

15. Profit rates play an important role, for example, in the equations explaining wage changes developd by Berry, by Schultze and Tryon, and by Eckstein and Wilson. See the references to their work in Note 18, Chapter 4.

16. As G. L. Perry points out, however, a sustained level of high employment, with neither spurts nor recessions in activity, should lead to a lower rate of profits than would exist during sporadic cyclical booms. G. L. Perry, *Unemployment, Money Wage Rates, and Inflation* (Cambridge, Massachusetts: M.I.T. Press, 1966), pp. 118–119; also pp. 112–114.

17. We leave aside the influence of raw material prices, particularly the prices of imported materials.

18. From July 1965 to July 1966, the CPI rose by 2.9 per cent. During this year, unemployment (seasonally adjusted) declined from 4.5 per cent in July 1965 to 3.7 per cent in February 1966 and then ranged between 3.7 and 4.0 per cent. A year is, of course, much too short a period for any inferences regarding long-run relationships. In addition, the price increase associated with an unemployment rate of 4 per cent, as unemployment declines rapidly from a higher figure, is not necessarily the rate of increase that would be associated with the steady maintenance of a 4 per cent rate. Other factors, of course, could also influence the behavior of prices; this includes the rate of change in labor productivity and the behavior of profits.

19. Paul A. Samuelson and Robert M. Solow, "Analytical Aspects of Anti-Inflation Policy," *American Economic Review: Papers and Proceedings*, L (May 1960), 192.

20. Perry, *op. cit.*, pp. 61–63, especially chart on p. 63. See also pp. 108–109. Similar calculations were made by C. L. Schultze and J. L. Tryon in their contribution to the Brookings model. As a first approximation they estimated that at 4 per cent unemployment and with profits at their 1948–1960 level, unit labor costs would rise by 1.5 to 2 per cent a year. However, such a rise in costs would lead to a rise in the CPI, which would raise wages further. Thus unemploymeent of 4 per cent would be associated with a rise in the price level of possibly somewhat more than 1.5 to 2 per cent. See their paper in J. S. Duesenberry et al., *The Brookings Quarterly Econometric Model of the United States* (Chicago: Rand McNally, 1965), pp. 329–330.

21. Although the evidence is subject to more than one interpretation, it would appear that the guideposts did have some modest restraining effect during 1962–1965. Thus the rate of wage increase during 1962–1965 was less than would have been predicted from the relationship between wage changes and unemployment (and other variables) in previous years. The evidence is less clear regarding prices, but here also I should judge that the guideposts did have a modest restraining effect. John Dunlop has expressed the view that the guideposts had some effect in restraining the rise in prices but no influence, beyond that already exerted by unemployment and other variables, on wages. See his paper in George P. Shultz and Robert Z. Aliber (eds.), *Guidelines, Informal Controls, and the Market Place* (Chicago: University of Chicago Press, 1966), pp. 83–84. Robert Solow, in the same volume (pp. 46–47) interprets the record in much the same fashion as I have.

22. For one retrospective defense of the guideposts by a man who helped to formulate them, see the statement by Kermit Gordon in Joint Economic Committee, *Twentieth Anniversary of the Employment Act of 1946: An Economic Symposium,* 89th Congress, 2nd Session (Washington: Government Printing Office, 1966), pp. 59–66. Paul McCracken takes a more cautious view in the same volume, pp. 67–76. For a range of views on the subject of the guideposts, see Shultz and Aliber (eds.), *op. cit.*

23. "A policy of sole reliance on demand-creating measures is certain to be more costly in terms of pressures on the price level than a dual attack through employment and manpower policies." Subcommittee on Employment and Manpower of the Senate Committee on Labor and Public Welfare, *op. cit.,* p. 30.

24. Strictly speaking, "labor market policy" is a broader term than "manpower policy," but we shall use the two interchangeably.

25. For a thoughtful and stimulating discussion of some of the questions considered here, see L. C. Thurow, "The Role of Manpower Policy in Achieving Aggregative Goals," in R. A. Gordon (ed.), *op. cit.,* Chap. 4.

26. Unfortunately, we can say little about the precise relation between a shift in the vacancies–unemployment relationship, such as that portrayed in Fig. 7.1, and the corresponding shift in the Phillips curve relating the rate of change in wages or prices to the level of unemployment. It is certain, however, that a shift to the left of the relationship (implying a decline in structural unemployment) will also lead the Phillips curve to shift to the left. In this connection, the reader should be reminded that our definition of full employment does not require that total vacancies equal total unemployment. See the discussion of this point in Chapter 4.

27. Various estimates exist as to the amount of frictional, including seasonal, unemployment. My own guess is that it is now in the neighborhood of 2 per cent, perhaps slightly more, of which seasonal unemployment represents perhaps one-third. Lester Thurow offers an estimate of 3 per cent, but he evidently includes some unemployment that I should call structural. See this paper, "The Role of Manpower Policy in Achieving Aggregative Goals," previously cited. See also Bureau of Labor Statistics, *The Extent and Nature of Frictional Unemployment,* Study Paper No. 6 in Joint Economic Committee, *Study of Employment, Growth, and Price Levels,* 86th Congress, 1st Session (Washington: Government Printing Office, 1959). Interestingly a recent Canadian study arrived at an estimate of 3 per cent for the "minimum unemployment" resulting from frictional, seasonal, and structural factors in Canada. Frank T. Denton and Sylvia Ostry, *An Analysis of Post-War Unemployment,* Staff Study No. 3, Economic Council of Canada (Ottawa: 1965).

28. See R. A. Gordon (ed.), *op. cit.,* Chapter 6; also R. A. Lester, *Manpower Planning in a Free Society* (Princeton: Princeton University Press, 1966).

29. The literature on American and foreign manpower policy has become too large to cite in any detail. In addition to the volumes cited in the preceding Note and the *Manpower Reports of the President,* mention might be made of the following: Subcommittee on Employment and Manpower of the Senate Committee on Labor and Public Welfare, *Toward Full Employment: Proposals for a Comprehensive Employment and Manpower Policy in the United States;* idem, *Selected Readings in Employment and Manpower* (Washington: Government Printing Office, 1964–1965), Vols. 4, 8, and 9; a series of volumes by OECD on manpower

programs in various countries; Margaret S. Gordon, *Retraining and Labor Market Adjustment in Western Europe* (Washington: Government Printing Office, 1965).

30. The anti-poverty program, dating from 1964, has provided for some direct public employment, for example, in the Job Corps, the Neighborhood Youth Corps, the Work Experience Program, and the Community Action Program. See, for example, Garth Mangum, "The Development of Manpower Policy, 1961–65," in Levitan and Siegel (eds.), *op. cit.,* p. 35.

31. This position has been taken by a number of others, of course, both in and out of Washington. In Chapter 3 we referred to the Clark Subcommittee's espousal of a 3 per cent rate by January 1968. For a more recent argument in favor of the 3 per cent goal, see Eleanor C. Gilpatrick, *Structural Unemployment and Aggregate Demand* (Baltimore: Johns Hopkins Press, 1966), Chap. 10.

32. For an interesting international study of the relation between unemployment and wage changes among a group of eight countries, see Joseph W. Garbarino, "Income Policy and Income Behavior," in A. M. Ross (ed.), *Employment Policy and the Labor Market* (Berkeley: University of California Press, 1965), pp. 56–88.

33. In a report prepared for the National Commission on Technology, Automation, and Economic Progress, G. L. Perry has estimated that an unemployment rate of 3.5 per cent would involve an increase of 2 to 2.5 per cent in the GNP deflator and that unemployment of 3 per cent would entail a rise in prices of 3 to 4 per cent a year. These estimates seem to assume continuation of manpower policies at approximately their present scale. Our estimate assumes an expanded set of manpower and labor market programs. Perry's report appears in the Commission's *The Outlook for Technological Change and Employment,* Appendix Volume 1 to *Technology and the American Economy* (Washington: Government Printing Office, 1966), pp. 193–202.

34. Indeed, by the fall of 1966, some were saying that the end had already come.

35. Compare the somewhat similar suggestions made by the President's Advisory Committee on Labor-Management Policy in its report issued in August 1966. For a useful evaluation of the guideposts and for some suggestions for making them more effective, see M. L. Joseph, "Requiem for a Lightweight: A Critical Historical Sketch," paper presented at a conference on *Pricing Theories, Practices, and Policies,* The Wharton School of Finance and Commerce, University of Pennsylvania, October 13, 1966.

36. See Report of the Subcommittee on Employment and Manpower of the Senate Committee on Labor and Public Welfare, *loc. cit.,* The Commission on Technology, Automation, and Economic Progress recommended "most strongly" that "economic policy aim resolutely and watchfully at a reduction in the general unemployment rate to 3.5 percent

or below by the beginning of 1967." *Technology and the American Economy,* p. 34.

37. Beyond our emphasis on maintaining aggregate demand and on a much expanded manpower program, we have not tried to spell out in detail the various ways in which we might try to move closer to the goal of 3 per cent. For more detailed proposals, the reader is referred to the Appendix, which produces the conclusions and recommendations of the National Commission on Technology, Automation, and Economic Progress in 1966.

38. In the words of the Council of Economic Advisers: "Although precise targets cannot be set for the ultimate minimum level of unemployment or the speed of the downward movement, it is clearly unnecessary and undesirable to accept 4-percent unemployment as a permanent objective of U.S. economic policy." *Economic Report of the President,* January 1967, p. 113.

APPENDIX

Summary of Major Conclusions and Recommendations of the National Commission on Technology, Automation, and Economic Progress[1]

The issues discussed in this report are complex and diverse. A brief summary of major conclusions cannot do justice to the report and is certainly not a substitute for the full text with its supporting evidence and argument. Once the text has been read, however, a summary may serve a useful purpose in crystallizing the major points and pointing up the recommendations which have been made. The principal conclusions and recommendations follow:

1. There has been some increase in the pace of technological change. The most useful measure of this increase for policy purposes is the annual growth of output per man-hour in the private economy. If 1947 is chosen as a dividing point, the trend rate of increase from 1909 to that date was 2 per cent per year; from 1947 to 1965 it was 3.2 per cent per year. This is a substantial increase, but there has not been and there is no evidence that there will be in the decade ahead an acceleration in tech-

[1] Reprinted from *Technology and the American Economy* (Washington: Government Printing Office, 1966), pp. 109–113.

nological change more rapid than the growth of demand can offset, given adequate public policies.

2. The excessive unemployment following the Korean war, only now beginning to abate, was the result of an economic growth rate too slow to offset the combined impact of productivity increase (measured in output per man-hour) and a growing labor force.

3. Since productivity is the primary source of our high standard of living and opportunity must be provided to those of the population who choose to enter the labor force, the growth of demand must assume the blame for and provide the answer to unemployment. But it must be realized that the growth rate required to match rising productivity and labor force growth rates is unprecedented in our history, though not in the history of other industrial economies. There will be a continuing need for aggressive fiscal and monetary policies to stimulate growth.

4. To say that technological change does not bear major responsibility for the general level of unemployment is not to deny the role of technological change in the unemployment of particular persons in particular occupations, industries, and locations. Economic and technological changes have caused and will continue to cause displacement throughout the economy. Technological change, along with other changes, determines who will be displaced. The rate at which output grows in the total economy determines the total level of unemployment and how long those who become unemployed remain unemployed, as well as how difficult it is for new entrants to the labor force to find employment.

5. Unemployment tends to be concentrated among those workers with little education, not primarily because technological developments are changing the nature of jobs, but because the uneducated are at the 'back of the line' in the competition for jobs. Education, in part, determines the employability and productivity of the individual, the adaptability of the labor force, the growth and vitality of the economy, and the quality of the society. But we need not await the slow process of education to solve the problem of unemployment.

6. The outlook for employment and adjustment to change in the next decade depends upon the policies followed. Uneven

growth and decline of occupations and industries could, but need not, cause serious difficulties for the economy as a whole. The number of unskilled jobs will not decline, though unskilled jobs will continue to as a proportion of all jobs. Growth patterns in both the economy and the labor force provide an important warning: Unless Negroes and, to a lesser degree, youth, are able to penetrate growing occupations and industries at a more rapid rate than in the past, their high unemployment rates will continue or even rise. Our society must do a far better job than it has in the past of assuring that the burdens of changes beneficial to society as a whole are not borne disproportionately by some individuals.

7. The more adequate fiscal policies of the past 2 years have proven their ability to lower unemployment despite continued technological change and labor force growth. Economic policy must continue, watchfully but resolutely, to reduce the general unemployment rate. We must never again present the spectacle of wartime prosperity and peacetime unemployment. The needs of our society are such that we should give major attention in our fiscal policies to public investment expenditures.

8. With the best of fiscal and monetary policies, there will always be those handicapped in the competition for jobs by lack of education, skill, or experience or because of discrimination. The needs of our society provide ample opportunities to fulfill the promise of the Employment Act of 1946: "a job for all those able, willing, and seeking to work." We recommend a program of public service employment, providing, in effect, that the Government be an employer of last resort, providing work for the "hard-core unemployed" in useful community enterprises.

9. Technological change and productivity are primary sources of our unprecedented wealth, but many persons have not shared in that abundance. We recommend that economic security be guaranteed by a floor under family income. That floor should include both improvements in wage-related benefits and a broader system of income maintenance for those families unable to provide for themselves.

10. To facilitate adjustment to change as well as to improve the quality of life, adequate educational opportunity should be

available to all. We recommend compensatory education for those from disadvantaged environments, improvements in the general quality of education, universal high school education and opportunity for 14 years of free public education, elimination of financial obstacles to higher education, lifetime opportunities for education, training, and retraining, and special attention to the handicaps of adults with deficient basic education.

11. Adjustment to change requires information concerning present and future job opportunities. We recommend the creation of a national computerized job–man matching system which would provide more adequate information on employment opportunities and available workers on a local, regional, and national scale. In addition to speeding job search, such a service would provide better information for vocational choice and alert the public and policymakers to impending changes.

12. The public employment service is a key instrument in adjustment to technological and economic changes. But it is presently handicapped by administrative obstacles and inadequate resources. We recommend the now federally financed but State-administered employment services be made wholly Federal. This would bring them into harmony with modern labor market conditions. Then they must be provided with the resources, both in manpower and funds, necessary to fulfill their crucial role.

13. We recommend that present experimentation with relocation assistance to workers and their families stranded in declining areas be developed into a permanent program.

14. Displacement, technological and otherwise, has been particularly painful to those blocked from new opportunity by barriers of discrimination. The Commission wishes to add its voice to others demanding elimination of all social barriers to employment and advocating special programs to compensate for centuries of systematic denial.

15. Technological and economic changes have differential geographic impacts requiring concerted regional efforts to take advantage of opportunities and avoid dislocation. We recommend that each Federal Reserve bank provide the leadership for economic development activities in its region. The development program in each Federal Reserve District should include: (1) A regular program of economic analysis; (2) an advisory council

for economic growth composed of representatives from each of the major interested groups within the district; (3) a capital bank to provide venture capital and long-term financing for new and growing companies; (4) regional technical institutes to serve as centers for disseminating scientific and technical knowledge relevant to the region's development; and (5) a Federal executive in each district to provide regional coordination of the various Federal programs related to economic development.

16. The responsibility of Government is to foster an environment of opportunity in which satisfactory adjustment to change can occur. But the adjustments themselves must occur primarily in the private employment relationship. The genius of the private adjustment process is the flexibility with which it accommodates to individual circumstances. Our report suggests areas for consideration by private and public employers, employees, and unions. We also recommend study of a reinsurance fund to protect pension rights and modifications of the investment tax credit to encourage employers to provide appropriate adjustment assistance. We also advocate a positive program by employers and unions to provide compensatory opportunities to the victims of past discrimination and stronger enforcement provisions in civil rights legislation relating to employment. Federal, State, and local governments are encouraged to conduct themselves as model employers in the development of new adjustment techniques.

17. Technology enlarges the capacities of man and extends his control over his environment. The benefits of increased productivity can and should be applied to combinations of higher living standards and increased leisure, improvements in the work environment, increased investment in meeting human and community needs, and assistance to less advantaged nations.

18. As examples of possible applications of new technologies to unmet human and community needs, we recommend improvements in health care, transportation, control of air and water pollution, and housing.

(1) To improve health care, we recommend: (a) Fuller access to diagnostic and patient care facilities by all groups

in the population; (b) broader and bolder use of the computer and other new health technologies; (c) increased spread and use of health statistics, information, and indexes; and (d) new programs for training health manpower.

(2) To aid the development of an efficient transportation system we recommend: Federal support of a systems research program directed toward (a) the problems of particular multi-state regions; (b) the determination of national transportation requirements, and (c) the evaluation of alternative programs.

(3) For air pollution control, we recommend: (a) Enlargement of research efforts to learn and understand the effects of various pollutants on living organisms; and (b) assignment of pollution costs to the sources of pollutants.

(4) To control water pollution, we recommend: The establishment of effective, amply empowered river basin authorities.

(5) To encourage improvement in housing technology, we recommend: (a) Federal stimulation of research; (b) use of federally supported public housing to provide initial markets for new housing technologies; (c) promulgation of a national model building code by making available Federal support and insurance of housing and other construction only in those communities which put their building codes in harmony with the national code; and (d) provision of adjustment assistance to any building crafts destroyed by technical change.

19. We also recommend (1) increased use of systems analysis in resolving social and environmental problems, (2) the use of Federal procurement as a stimulus to technological innovation through purchasing by performance criteria rather than product specification, (3) provision of Federal funds to universities and other organizations for the improvement of research techniques and their experimental application to urban problems, (4) the formation of university institutes integrated with the educational function which would serve as laboratories for urban problem analysis and resources for local communities wanting their advice and services, and (5) increased efforts to make available for non-government use results of Government performed or funded research.

20. Finally, we recommend: (1) Efforts by employers to "hu-

manize" the work environment by (a) adapting work to human needs, (b) increasing the flexibility of the lifespan of work, and (c) eliminating the distinction in the mode of payment between hourly workers and salaried employees; (2) exploration of a system of social accounts to make possible assessment of the relative costs and benefits of alternative policy decisions; and (3) continuous study of national goals and evaluation of our national performance in relation to such goals.

Index